THE BOOK OF

WHEAT WEAVING
AND STRAW CRAFT

Morgyn Geoffry Owens-Celli

THE BOOK OF

WHEAT WEAVING
AND STRAW CRAFT

FROM

Simple Plaits

TO

Exquisite
Designs

Morgyn Geoffry Owens-Celli

Lark Books

This book is dedicated to Frank V. Fox IV and to my parents, Jackie and Lowell.
Without their support, it might never have been written.

Editor: Chris Rich

Art and Production: Elaine Thompson and Bobby Gold

Illustrator: Kelley Jones

Principle photographer: Evan Bracken

Additional photography: Michael G. Patton

Library of Congress Cataloging-in-Publication Data
Owens-Celli, Morgyn Geoffry, 1952–
     The book of wheat weaving and straw craft : from simple plaits to
exquisite designs / by Morgyn Geoffry Owens-Celli.
          p.   cm.
     Includes index.
     ISBN 1-887374-20-5
     1. Straw work.   2. Grass weaving.   I. Title.
TT876.O94   1997
746.41--dc20   96-35514
                                                                        CIP

10 9 8 7 6 5 4 3 2 1

Published in 1997 by Lark Books
50 College Street
Asheville, North Carolina, U.S.A. 28801

© 1997 by Morgyn Geoffry Owens-Celli

Distributed in the U.S. by Sterling Publishing,
     387 Park Ave. South, New York, NY 10016; 1-800-367-9692

Distributed in Canada by Sterling Publishing, c/o Canadian Manda Group,
     One Atlantic Avenue, Suite 105, Toronto, Ontario, Canada M6K 3E7

Distributed in Great Britain and Europe by Cassell PLC,
     Wellington House, 125 Strand, London, England WC2R OBB

Distributed in Australia by Capricorn Link (Australia) Pty Ltd.,
     P.O. Box 6651, Baulkham Hills Business Centre, NSW 2153, Australia

The projects in this book which are the creations of the author and contributing
artists may be reproduced by individuals for personal pleasure; reproduction on a
larger scale with the intent of personal profit is prohibited. Copyrights to original
designs are retained by the designers.

Every effort has been made to ensure that all information in this book is accurate.
However, due to differing conditions, tools, and individual skills, the publisher
cannot be responsible for any injuries, losses, or other damages which may result
from the use of the information in this book.

Printed in Hong Kong

ISBN 1-887374-20-5

Opposite page

Top:
Black Forest Crown
KELLEY JONES

Bottom:
Country Favor
MORGYN OWENS-CELLI

Contents

Introduction

Ask wheat weavers why they love this ancient folk art, and you'll get more answers than you thought possible. Why? Because the community you're about to join is as varied in taste and temperament, in ethnic and economic background, in education and experience as any craft community in existence. Its members—old and young, rich and poor—practice their craft from Egypt to Lithuania, England to Japan, and Ireland to the United States.

Some weavers are captivated by this craft's direct ties to some of civilization's oldest beliefs and rituals. These are the men and women who savor recreating ancient designs such as the Moroccan Cage, with which Egyptians once hoped to capture the spirit of the grain between one year's harvest and the next.

Others are simply continuing a tradition that has thrived in their families for generations: the French family whose forbears celebrated vineyard harvests by weaving straw designs; the English woman or man whose great-grandmother once wove ornaments for the Royal Family; the Lithuanian who couldn't imagine a wedding without the gift of a straw songbird.

Many weavers start out as nature-oriented hobbyists and choose wheat weaving because they love working with a natural material—one that's beautiful, relatively inexpensive, and safe to use.

Still others are hooked by the fact that both beginners and experts are welcome within the world of this folk art. Wheat weaving offers a huge array of designs—from incredibly simple but lovely individual plaits to projects so challenging that museums vie to display them.

Craftspeople who'd rather think of themselves as hobbyists than artists are often relieved to discover that while wheat weaving certainly invites creativity, it's not a craft that demands it. Literally hundreds of stunning, easy-to-make designs already exist; once you've learned the basic plaits, you'll never run short of weavings to make. But who knows? As your skills and confidence increase, you may want to join the ranks of contemporary artists who love creating their own designs. Just as suitors used to pride themselves on creating distinctive straw Love Knots for their sweethearts, many of today's weavers derive their satisfaction from coming up with new plaits and new ways to incorporate them in larger projects.

We're willing to bet that no matter who you are—nature crafter or historian, fiber artist or weekend hobbyist—and no matter what you expect from a craft—a relaxing pastime or a life's vocation—you'll find something compelling about working with wheat. This book has been written for all of you. Welcome to the world of wheat weaving!

Unless you're already an expert wheat weaver (and we'll talk to those of you who are in a minute), you'll get more from this book if you focus first on Chapters One, Two, and Three, reading them carefully, a bit at a time, and in sequence. We don't mean to discourage browsing; by all means take a visual tour through the entire book, but keep in mind that the projects in the last few chapters will be easier and more enjoyable to make if you learn the basics first.

How to Use This Book

Chapter One will introduce you to a bit of the history and folklore surrounding this craft and will lend to every project you make the special understanding that comes only when a weaver knows the origins of the design he or she is creating.

Chapter Two will walk you through preparing your materials, gathering the necessary tools, and learning the six hand positions most frequently used in wheat weaving.

Chapter Three will guide you through making the basic plaits—individual weaves that are often combined to make more sophisticated projects. Practice by weaving at least one of every plait presented; they're all beautiful, they all make wonderful gifts, and they'll all help you develop and practice good weaving techniques. This chapter is also loaded with tips to improve your weaving and make it more enjoyable.

Chapters Four through Eight offer more sophisticated designs. You can skip around in these chapters as you like, but do start with less challenging projects and progress to more complex designs as your skills increase. You'll find explanations of the "Challenge Rating" symbols on page 55.

Chapter Nine includes instructions for making a variety of straw embellishments for your projects, including stars, bows, and coils.

If you're already a skilled wheat weaver, browse through the project photos, select a design that appeals to you, and begin! If your project includes a plait you've never learned, take a look at the "Techniques" list that comes with the project instructions; it will tell you where to find the information you need.

Opposite page:

Circle of Hearts
LINDA MEEKER

Above:

Easter Medallion (contemporary Russian wheat weaving)
Courtesy of the American Museum of Straw Art

1

The History of Wheat Weaving

Wheat has been of tremendous importance to mankind since Neolithic man first included it in his cave drawings and buried it with his dead—important as a foodstuff, of course, but more significantly, as a symbol for thousands upon thousands of years of people's highest hopes and deepest fears. Wheat weaving—an art form with origins almost as old as wheat itself—embodies the grain-related beliefs, rituals, and customs of many centuries and many cultures.

American Straw Purse (circa 1880)
Courtesy of the American Museum of Straw Art

Although the first efforts to cultivate wheat were probably made by nomadic farmers in the Middle and Near East around 8000 B.C., perhaps the oldest actual evidence of wheat cultivation comes from Egyptian drawings of grain fields. These date back five thousand years, to about the time the plow was invented.

We do know of myths that predate this evidence, however, including that of the goddess Isis. According to this myth, wheat grew wild on the slopes of the Nile Valley, where it was cultivated and harvested exclusively by women. Not until Isis taught her husband Osiris these activities was this once sacred female domain shared with men. The earth-mother cult that developed around Isis was one of the earliest in which grain played an important part in worship and symbolism.

Remains of Egyptian clay pots from this era are impressed with designs made with wheat and plaited straw, and Egyptian tomb drawings depict what appear to be woven bundles of wheat on harvest tables. Why this straw work was created is the subject of some debate. The designs and drawings may simply represent plaited bindings that kept bundles of straw intact, but some historians postulate that the woven wheat had a more important symbolic purpose, one deeply rooted in beliefs of that time.

Most ancient cultures were ignorant of farming theory, so their agricultural myths and customs focused on the fear of crop failure and the desire for successful harvests. In many cultures, including that of the Egyptians, the belief in a spirit or god who lived in the grain and whose home was destroyed each time the grain was harvested was a strong one. Wheat weavings may have originated as a method of providing a temporary home (or trap) for this god of the field. By weaving the last of each harvest into an ornament or cage, the farmer could house or imprison the god until the next planting, when the ornament—and god within—were returned to the soil. (Today, a North African wheat weaving known as a "cage" is still reproduced in modern Egypt.) Wheat weavings also celebrated the present year's harvest, of course, but more important, they ensured the success of the next.

Greeks who visited Egypt (the Greek pantheon also included a wheat deity) wrote of "great ritual" connected with the Egyptian harvest but never mentioned wheat-woven ornaments. It's possible that these early Greek chroniclers simply overlooked the humble harvest custom of weaving wheat, but it's more likely that this folk art had already spread from Egypt to the Mediterranean world, so the familiar weavings simply did not strike Greek visitors as noteworthy.

In early Greek mythology, wheat became associated with the goddess of agriculture, Demeter, whose name means "wheat-giver," and hence with the concept of motherhood. Woven wheat puppets made in her honor were used at festivals to convey some of the ancient mysteries connected with the cycles of growth exemplified by the grain.

Woman's Straw Hat (early 1900s)
Courtesy of the American Museum of Straw Art

In Rome, the goddess of the fields was Ceres, from whose name the word "cereal" is derived. Many drawings, sculptures, and accounts of the time bear witness to a type of woven straw tribute made for her and displayed on lavish harvest tables. Her favorite flowers, red poppies, which were thought to bring good luck, were grown along with the wheat, and red ribbons were often tied to the straw ornaments as further tributes. In fact, the red ribbon adornments still found on straw ornaments from various cultures may be relics of this ancient practice.

As the Roman Empire spread, so did its customs and ritual artifacts, and there is little doubt that the straw tributes to Ceres were among them. In time, these wheat tributes and the concepts underlying their origins blended with the customs and rituals of the conquered northern European "barbaric" tribes. These tribes believed in a wheat spirit rather than in a goddess of the grain—a spirit more personal than the deities of the Roman pantheon and one to whom clans, families, or individuals could relate.

Although some aspects of Roman life and culture remained after the fall of the Roman Empire, local traditions once again came to the fore. The broad agricultural experience that Rome had brought to its outposts was gradually lost; local superstitions and customs dominated methods of planting and harvesting wheat. As a result, during the period that extended from the end of the western Roman Empire to the beginning of the Middle Ages, wheat cultivation suffered. Because farmers often did not know why their crops had failed, they came to rely heavily on old-wives' tales for explanations and on ancient customs and rituals for solutions.

American Straw Purse (circa 1870)
Courtesy of the American Museum of Straw Art

The focus of these tales and rituals was the difficult task of appeasing the spirit that inhabited the wheat—a spirit that could be angered by farming methods, failure to observe proper rituals, unevenly plowed rows, harvesting equipment not properly blessed, and even the temperament of one's plowing horses.

Every aspect of planting and harvesting was therefore carefully orchestrated. In many European villages, the correct time for planting was determined by bringing the oldest and most venerated man of the village out into the fields. Placed ceremoniously on the ground, he would determine whether or not the soil was warm enough for sowing seed; his "hindsight" was greatly respected. In other areas, planting customs were often related to the rising or setting of specific constellations. In England, for example, winter wheat was planted at the setting of the Pleiades and harvested shortly after its rise during the following spring or summer season. The seasons of the earth did not always match celestial patterns, however, so farmers in some areas relied upon local weather folklore instead.

Plowing fields for winter wheat was carried out with characteristic caution. In some locales, children or young women started this task by moonlight, in the belief that evil spirits could not harm them when it was dark. At daylight, when the spirits had been tricked into moving on to other fields, adult males would finish the plowing. Some farmers believed that walking the plow backwards would fool these evil spirits. Others disguised themselves by wearing costumes, which could be shed along with any bad luck that might befall the wearers.

Woman's Dyed Straw Hat (circa 1890)
Courtesy of the American Museum of Straw Art

Harvest rituals and customs were just as important as those related to planting. These customs differed vastly, even within particular European enclaves, but for all their differences, similar themes ran through them. Each year, a group of reapers known as "harvest lads" travelled from south to north, harvesting wheat as it ripened in the fields of one area and then moving on to the next. These reapers brought with them the harvest rituals they believed would ensure good yields and prevent bad weather from ruining the crop.

The reapers believed that as a field was harvested, the spirit of the grain jumped from sheaf to sheaf until it reached the last section to be cut. In order not to incur the spirit's wrath when this section was harvested (a wrath that could cause great harm to befall the unfortunate victim), a group of lads would cut the final section together so that the spirit could not single out an individual culprit. This group effort was known as "cutting in common." The last bit of wheat—and the spirit trapped in it—was then shaped into a weaving and kept until the next crop was planted.

Straw Appliqué Ark

Made in 1799 in Tunbridge Wells, England, this piece may have been created by French prisoners of war during Napoleon's regime.

Courtesy of the American Museum of Straw Art

Photo courtesy of photographer Michael G. Patton

Sullivan Box (mid 1700s)

This appliquéd jewelry box was made in the mid 1700s as a courting gift. The flowers in its design offer symbolic promises of love, faith, and passion, and the ships reflect the interests of the original owner— a wine merchant who traded overseas.

Courtesy of the American Museum of Straw Art

Photo courtesy of photographer Michael G. Patton

This custom was best preserved in Devon, England, where the reapers simultaneously threw their sickles at the last of the wheat, which was then woven into a long spiral design called a "neck." One of the harvest lads would grab the neck and call out, "I have it, I have it," to which the others would respond, "What have you?" The lad would reply, "The neck, the neck, the neck!" He would then run as fast as he could to the farm house. If he managed to enter it before the prettiest maiden of the farm could tag him, he was rewarded with a kiss. If the maiden caught him first, she doused him with water.

This quaint ritual, which survived into the beginning of the twentieth century, was based on ancient folklore. The neck itself was a totem representing an animal, perhaps a goose that in centuries past might have been sacrificed for the harvest feast. The dousing with water was probably related to an ancient rite carried out to prevent rain from spoiling the harvest. (Rain-prevention rituals were once common. Scythes and sickles were often cleansed with water for just this purpose, and during the Renaissance, local vicars would often sprinkle farm implements with holy water for the same reason.)

After the harvest, the wheat weaving that housed the spirit of the grain was hung safely in a place of honor, usually in the home, until the next planting, when the spirit was

Swiss Straw Lace Element for the Hat Industry (mid 1800s)
Courtesy of the American Museum of Straw Art

What did ancient wheat weavings look like? There are two schools of thought. Some historians believe that the ornaments looked like stacks of wheat, resembling female figures, in the fields and that these represented either the earth mother or the wheat spirit herself. Other historians suggest that the earliest weavings were spirals, sometimes called "drop dollies" today because their spiral plaits open, or drop, to form a wide base before closing. These spirals, under different names, appear in many cultures throughout Eurasia and Africa. They're considered by some to be the oldest wheat weavings known and may represent attempts to trap the wheat spirit.

Ancient beliefs regarding the spiral shape itself are quite fascinating. In many cultures, for example, people thought that walking backwards or in a spiral pattern would prevent the harm that might result from having made a mistake. These same movements were also thought to imprison or banish evil spirits and are common in many superstitions. You're probably familiar with at least a couple of these: If you walk under a ladder, walking backwards from under it will prevent bad luck; and if you spill salt, you can rectify the situation by throwing salt over your left shoulder—in the opposite direction from the spill.

returned to the soil to create a new home for herself and a successful harvest for the farmer. In order not to anger the spirit, some farmers threw the weaving over the scythes and sickles to land in the field, where it could then be plowed under to release the spirit into the soil. In other areas, the wheat weaving was placed in the center of the field and blessed by the local priest or clergyman. In yet others, the weaving was fed to the plow-horse team. As the horses worked, the spirit wended her way through their equine innards and out into the soil.

Wheat weavings were made from the best of the year's harvest and demonstrated the farmer's pride in his finest grain. In fact, some of the oldest seeds remaining in museum wheat weavings represent a history of the weather and seed quality for the year in which the wheat was woven. These weavings are also seed banks for the future, as the ornaments were sometimes made with types of wheat no longer grown.

Harvest rituals and celebrations involved the tools, harvesters, and community as a whole. The last load of wheat was brought home in a cart to which the farm tools were attached with ribbons and wheat weavings. Atop this "last load" wagon rode the "harvest queen" and, in some areas, a plow boy or "harvest lord," who were hosts of the harvest celebrations. The queen ruled amidst such activities as sickle dancing and sat at the head of a harvest table that could have rivaled that of any Roman feast. The new wheat weaving occupied a prominent place on the table.

Somerset Apple and Flagon (1954)
GEORGE DABINETT
Courtesy of the American Museum of Straw Art

American Straw Purse (circa 1850)
Courtesy of the American Museum of Straw Art

Whether the earliest weavings were spiral cages or stacks of wheat woven to represent female forms, their designs were simple and varied little for thousands of years. If it's difficult to believe that an art form could remain static for such a long time, given the rapidly changing world we live in, keep in mind how few external forces influenced day-by-day existence in ancient times.

As travel and trade increased after the Middle Ages, shared knowledge helped to improve farming techniques, and crops started to improve. Harvest failures gradually became the exception rather than the rule, and harvest celebrations, with all their cherished traditions, increased. Wheat weavings continued to play a role in these celebrations and rituals, but the cultural purpose they once filled—housing the spirit of the wheat—became less apparent.

Wheat weaving gradually came to be viewed as an integral part of the rich heritage of harvest-related activities and beliefs of rural peoples. Perhaps no other symbol was as laden with meaning for farmers of the time. As a result, weaving became a competitive activity in which individuals vied to make the weaving that would be selected as the official village design or that would be displayed on the grand harvest table. Certainly by the eighteenth century and perhaps as early as the sixteenth, most of the designs we now identify as traditional had appeared. The

"neck" design remained and was embellished upon, and other designs, representing farm tools or the earth itself, developed.

In Britain, wheat weavings were called "corn dollies." ("Corn" is a generic term for grain or kernel, and "dolly" is a corruption of the word "idol"—hence, "corn dolly" means grain idol.) Individual English counties developed distinctive designs. In Suffolk, for example, where horses were abundant, the traditional design was a horseshoe. In Kent, where the Ivy Wine Festivals were held, the Ivy Girl of Kent was the representative pattern.

Wheat ornaments were now made not only for harvest celebrations, but also as courting favors, to commemorate special events, as a means of marking calendar seasons or dates, and as religious symbols. Courting favors—wheat-woven love tokens—are probably among the most widespread of traditional wheat weavings. Because an abundance of wheat had always been associated with good fortune, wheat made the perfect material for a hopeful suitor. Even today, some people believe that a courtship started in a wheat field will yield the finest love and greatest happiness.

These favors were generally simple in design and could be woven at a moment's notice. A favorite pastime for harvesters was to plait simple braids for their sweethearts in the hope that their affection would be returned. Worn over a maiden's heart, the braid served to let others know that her love had been successfully claimed by the weaver of that plait. Because individual suitors obviously wanted their courting favors to identify them clearly, a tremendous number of designs were developed.

In East Anglia, a lad who wished to court his sweetheart would be given some wheat when he visited her. He was only permitted to be alone with her as he wove it, on the assumption that his hands would be kept too busy to wander elsewhere. If the courtship was successful, the "courting knot" that he'd made was displayed on the wedding altar and was later transferred to the young couple's home in order to promote both fertility and good fortune. Courting-knot designs were often quite intricate, as suitors wished to impress their sweethearts with their ability to work with their hands—especially important at a time and place when so many necessities of life were handmade.

"Commemoratives," created to celebrate specific times or events, make up another category of traditional wheat weavings. The Easter Cross is one obvious example. The Ivy Girl of Kent, made to commemorate the Ivy Wine Festivals, is another. Guy Fawkes Day Dolls were made and burned in bonfires to commemorate the day upon which this famous English conspirator was caught in an attempt to blow up King James I and

Woman's Straw Hat (circa 1889)
RESTYLED BY JENNIFER LANDON
Courtesy of the American Museum of Straw Art

manipulate, and because farmers wished to offer public proof of the fine quality of their harvests.

By the nineteenth century, wheat weaving had become a mainstay of the straw hat and bonnet industry. Hundreds of Ribbon plaits, for example, were developed in order to create distinctive straw headware, and businesses thrived on coming up with new wheat-woven patterns. Popular designs were often patented, and some, such as the very common Dunstable plait (see page 39), were also named for the towns in which the businesses were located.

Although wheat weaving has evolved from its origins into an art form less steeped in ritual, today's weavings have changed surprisingly little over the centuries. When the contemporary weaver works on a Devonshire Neck or a North African Cage, he or she may be repeating the same steps taken by a wheat weaver hundreds of years ago. Yet wheat weaving is also a growing folk art to which new designs are added all the time.

Today's weavers are attracted to this art form for a multitude of reasons. Some love the natural quality of the material. In our modern age of machines, displaying a part of what nature provides makes our homes cozier and warmer. Others are fascinated by the culture and folk history that distinguish the traditional plaits and braids of one culture from another. Still others find that this art form, unlike many others, provides an open invitation to creativity; ancient and contemporary designs walk hand-in-hand. Perhaps the true romance of wheat weaving is its power to give expression— as it has for so many centuries—to the hopes and artistic inclinations of so many different people.

the Parliament. In Lithuania, the three-dimensional star was originally made to commemorate the appearance of the Star of Bethlehem, and in time, straw work became a national symbol. The Czechoslovakian Straw Man was probably a traditional Easter commemorative, and in Poland, emblems and shields were made to honor important individuals or towns. In France, woven designs were created to celebrate grape harvests.

Better farming techniques and more abundant harvests, combined with an increased sense of national identity and pride, led many countries to officially sanction what had once been a primitive harvest ritual. The recognition of this country art form by the Church of England in 1751 is an excellent example.

Wheat weaving was now viewed as both a charming example of local country crafts and as a significant aspect of rural culture. Weavers competed to have their work displayed in churches during harvest festival celebrations, when parishes displayed religious ornaments or county designs. These competitions created a new enthusiasm for wheat weaving and were largely responsible for helping it make the transition from rural craft and folk ritual to the highest level of folk art.

For several reasons, the quality of straw work gradually improved. The most obvious is that intricate designs served to display the weaver's skill. In addition, the weavings were made with the best quality wheat both because complex designs couldn't be made with coarse wheat, which is difficult to

Purl-Plait Man's Hat (circa 1960s)
Courtesy of the American Museum of Straw Art

2

Preparations

Preparing your materials in advance, making good use of your tools, and monitoring your own progress will improve your work and make it more enjoyable. Learning the essentials first will also allow you to make creative choices later. You can't go wrong if you follow the instructions and suggestions in this book, but you'll find ample room for your own creativity, too. The recommendations as to which varieties of wheat to use for specific projects, for example, aren't written in stone. Likewise, if you discover hand positions for wheat weaving that are more comfortable than the ones described in this chapter, by all means use them.

Selecting Grains

Theoretically, straws from any number of grains can be woven. Why is wheat the most commonly used and which varieties are best? More than fifty thousand wheat varieties exist, each different in size, color, texture, strength, durability, ease of plaiting, and artistic effect.

Many wheat varieties, however, and many other grains as well, are unsuitable for plaiting and are commercially unavailable, so your choices are narrower than you might think.

Left to right: Barley, rye, oats, rice, bearded Plains wheat, beardless wheat, black bearded wheat

Barley

Few varieties of this grain are suitable for straw work and most are difficult to find. Their *awns*—the long hairlike spikes emanating from the heads—are silky and extremely fragile, and their short, thick-walled straws make the plaiting process a struggle at best. Some straw artists use barley and similar, stronger grains in projects that don't require weaving.

Rye

Much traditional Scandinavian work is made with rye, which grows plentifully in that area of the world. Most varieties—both bearded and beardless—are longer than wheat, so the straws were once popular with straw hat and bonnet industries around the world. Rye, however, can be difficult to find; floral suppliers are often a good bet.

Some commercial ryes are harvested green and freeze-dried to help retain their pale green color. Although these will work for plaiting, rye that is commercially harvested tends to have short, thick straws and works best in designs such as the Welsh Fan and Corizon (see pages 58 and 64), where long straws aren't always necessary.

Avoid rye varieties that have been dyed or treated with bleach. Exposure to sunlight will turn green rye blonde within a few years anyway. If you'd like to leach the natural green color from the rye yourself, try soaking the stalks in scalding hot water.

Oats

A beautiful and gentle-looking grain, with V-shaped seed pods that fall in graceful clusters from center stems, oats are sometimes used for plaiting, but few varieties will survive the test of time. Their seed pods break off too easily. The pods of early-harvested oats are slightly stronger, but all oats are essentially fragile.

Use oats as a decorative element to add texture to your work, placing them, for example, at the base of a design. The very soft straws also add attractive pearly-white accents to appliqué work (see page 21).

Rice

Common in many Asian weavings, this delicate-looking grain with its full, wispy head, presents a range of color and texture unlike that of any other grain. Unfortunately, rice today is harvested with machinery that pulls the seeds from the plants, leaving little material with which to work. Few commercial sources exist for early-harvest rice, but it is available from a few floral outlets. If you live in a rice-growing region, harvest the rice about a week after the paddy has been drained, when the plants are still green at the top and the golden leaves emerge only at the base.

Wheat

This grain is by far the best for straw work. Wheat varieties come with and without beards and in many colors and textures and are available through commercial suppliers (see page 140). Varieties differ in size and diameter, although all wheats will have a mix of sizes within their yield.

If you wish to grow your own wheat, your local agricultural department may help you locate sources, select varieties for your area, and provide harvesting advice. Tell the personnel there that you're looking for long-stemmed varieties with heads of average length. (Older varieties will often be best.) The agricultural department at a local university may also be helpful, and libraries sometimes have information on where to buy seed.

Wheat must be harvested during the dough stage, just after the seed will exude a milky substance when squeezed and before the grain has matured. The straw should be golden at the top and green at the base. Cut small quantities by hand; for larger quantities, machinery will help considerably. Cut and bind bundles without crushing or destroying the material. Let the straws dry completely; you'll soak them before you begin weaving.

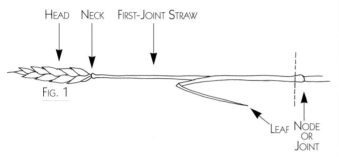

Figure 1 shows the various parts of a piece of wheat. The *head*, which contains the seeds, has a good deal of texture and color. The *neck* (or stem) is the short portion that connects the head to the *straw* and is solid rather than hollow. Several *nodes* (or joints) interrupt the hollow straw, and the leaves extend from them. Because hollow material is easier to weave than solid material, the part you'll weave is the *first-joint straw*—the section between the neck and the first of these nodes. *Second-joint straw* (the portion between the first and second nodes) is most often used as a core around which first-joint straw is woven.

Beginners who wish to order their wheat from a mail-order supplier will find that three general varieties of wheat are commonly available:

Plains Wheat

Grown in the Plains wheat belt of North America, this variety has delicate, soft straws, making it an easy-to-manipulate wheat for beginners, but one which doesn't hold its shape quite as well as thicker-walled wheat varieties. Plains wheat will make wonderfully flexible, flat Ribbon plaits, for example, but won't work as well for Spirals, which require a stiffer variety in order to maintain their three-dimensional shapes.

Black Bearded Wheat

Dramatic in color and texture, this wheat has thicker straw walls than other varieties. Manipulating its stiff straws does take a bit more practice than bending the straws of a softer

Left to right: Plains wheat, black bearded wheat, and beardless wheat

Plains wheat, but the results make extra learning time well worthwhile. You'll find that the bends and folds you make with black bearded wheat are crisper, cleaner-looking, and longer-lasting than those made with softer varieties.

Beardless Wheat

Usually golden in color and less visually complex that bearded varieties, the beardless wheats lend their own special look to any project in which they're used.

In the United States, wheat for weaving is generally sold by the pound (453.6 g). One or two pounds will be all you need to practice the basic plaits described in the next chapter.

Preparing Wheat for Weaving

Dry wheat can't be woven, as it's far too brittle to bend without breaking. Before you begin any project, you must sort and soak the wheat.

Sorting and Grading

For some projects, your straws must be graded and sorted

according to their diameters and the sizes of their heads. Plaiting with straws of widely different diameters will make your work uneven because the larger straws will push smaller ones out of position.

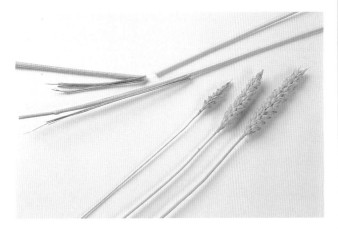

Removing Leaves

Because leaves prevent straws from absorbing water, you must remove them before soaking the straws. Use scissors to cut the straw just above the first node and slide off the leaves, or hold the head in one hand and, with other hand, bend the straw at a right angle just above the first node. This will break the straw inside the leaf without breaking the leaf itself. Pull sharply, and the leaf and remaining straw will come off, leaving just the head and first-joint straw.

Soaking

Count out the required straws for a particular project and make sure they've been sorted correctly before you soak them. (It never hurts to prepare a few more than you need.)

Place the straws in a soaking container filled with hot water, immersing them completely but being careful not to bend them. To keep them from floating, either weigh them down with ceramic tiles or wrap them in a towel first.

Soaking times vary greatly from grain to grain and among varieties. The thicker the walls of the straws, the more time they'll need. Black bearded wheat, for example, takes about four hours to soak. A blonde-headed wheat such as a Plains wheat takes only about thirty to forty minutes. To test any variety, soak a single straw for thirty minutes. If it feels bouncy and flexible, it's probably ready. If it cracks when you try to bend it, let it soak longer. Commercial suppliers of wheat for weaving should know the suggested soaking times for the varieties they sell.

Oversoaking and resoaking wheat can discolor the straw, turning it a brassy, mustard yellow instead of its characteristics blonde. If your wheat is badly molded or has been severely discolored by previous soaking, you may want to use diluted or undiluted white wine vinegar instead of water. Rinse the vinegar-soaked wheat thoroughly, as the acidic vinegar may cause long-term problems with the straw.

Keeping the Straws Damp

When working outdoors, cover the soaked straws with a damp cloth so that the sun and wind don't dry them out. If you need to take a break, wrap the damp straw in a plastic bag and place it in the freezer, where the moisture level will remain constant. When you're ready to resume, just run the straws under hot water to melt the ice crystals.

Customary Knots for Wheat Weaving

Plaits are often started by tying two or more straws together just below their necks. (As you can see in Figures 2 and 3, the position of the neck will vary slightly with each wheat variety.) The best knot for this purpose and for tying together the plaited parts of more complex projects, is the clove hitch (Fig. 4).

Sometimes you'll manipulate straws around a core consisting of a bundle of straws, a straw-covered wire, or a bare wire. When two cores must be tied

FIG. 2   FIG. 3

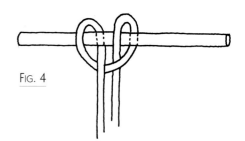

FIG. 4

together, the scaffold knot (Fig. 5) works best, especially in God's Eye designs (see pages 74-75). This knot will help maintain the correct angles between the arms of the cores.

FIG. 5

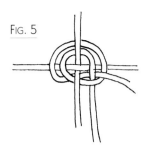

Preparing Wheat for Appliqué Work

Straw appliqué (also known as *marquetry, straw mosaic, or straw inlay*) is another form of straw art, one in which straws are split open, ironed flat, and glued to a backing such as heavy paper or wood in order to display their brilliant, flattened exteriors. Although preparing *splits* of straw for appliqué work takes a bit of practice, the results are well worth the effort.

Determining whether or not a straw is suitable for appliqué work isn't easy. Beardless varieties are usually the most suitable, but any variety can be adversely affected by weather or harvesting problems. Relatively large-diameter straws with walls that aren't too thick are best. To test any variety, soak a straw, split it open, and flatten it out to make sure it's 3/16" to 5/16" (4.5 to 7.5 mm) wide and 10" to 14" (25.4 to 35.6 cm) long. Straw varieties that split irregularly, breaking across their lengths, aren't suitable for appliqué.

To make splits of straw, cut off the heads and soak the straws as usual. Hold a soaked straw at the thick (bottom)

Straw Appliqué Cross (and detail)
JIMMY TRUJILLO (Albuquerque, New Mexico)
Courtesy of the American Museum of Straw Art

end and insert the blade of a small pair of scissors or a craft knife into the hollow stem (Fig. 6).

FIG. 6

Cut the straw open along its length. Using a needle or crochet hook, open up the curled edges at one end (Fig. 7) and insert the tip of an iron set for silk or linen (Fig. 8). Iron the inside of the straw until the material is dry and fully flat. For good measure, turn the straw over and iron once on the outer surface. Make sure your steam setting is off, or the iron will remoisten the material.

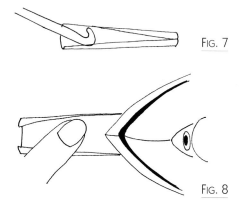

FIG. 7

FIG. 8

Each split has two sides: the *satin* (or outer) layer and the *starch* (or inner) layer, which contains the thick, spongy pith. The starchy pith is extremely absorbent and sometimes holds glue in an irregular fashion. In order to ensure even gluing and maintain a flat surface in the finished work, de-pith the starch side by cutting or scraping off some of the starch with a craft knife or razor blade. Work the knife or blade at an angle so that it removes some of the pith without cutting into the split. For instructions on how to use splits in appliqué work, turn to pages 125-126.

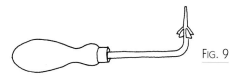

FIG. 9

Very narrow straw splits are used to make delicate ornaments as well as thin covers to hide thread ties. You may use a *splitter*—the only tool specific to wheat weaving (Fig. 9)— to make these narrow splits. The pointed end of the tool is inserted into the straw and its cutting flutes split the straw into a given number of lengths, each the same width. (Different splitters come with different numbers of flutes.)

Preparing to Dry Finished Projects

The damp straws in a finished project will assume a permanent shape once they've dried, so positioning the project carefully before drying it is very important.

If a damp project can be shaped by hand and the straws don't resist your efforts to arrange them as you like, the best way to dry the project is on a piece of screen positioned horizontally and above the floor or ground. Because adequate air circulation and quick, even drying are essential, placing the screen and project outdoors in sunlight works best, but leaving the screen indoors and turning on a nearby fan is also effective.

Some projects will require more shaping than a gentle prod here and there can provide. In order to hold these projects in position as they dry, you'll need to shape them as desired and then pin them onto a sheet of rigid polystyrene foam or cardboard. (Avoid solid surfaces such as wood or metal. These may cause the wheat to "sweat" as it dries, discoloring the wheat surfaces in contact with them.)

No matter which drying method you use, do be sure to arrange the project parts with care, fanning out any wheat heads to display their graceful forms.

Gathering Your Tools, Materials, and Supplies

You'll probably find that you already own most if not all of the tools and supplies for wheat weaving. Take a good look at the lists that follow and collect what you need before you begin.

Basic Tools and Supplies

~ Straw-soaking tubs, which can range from simple wallpaper tubs to heavy plastic flower boxes. Select tubs long enough to accommodate the longest wheat varieties you use.

~ Regular-sized scissors

~ Small scissors with delicate blades

~ Ruler

~ Thread, which must be strong and must not lose its tensile strength when wet. The most suitable—unwaxed three-comb linen thread—is available through upholstery and leather-work suppliers. Synthetic carpet threads and strong commercial cottons are acceptable alternatives, and unwaxed dental floss will work in a pinch. Test your selected thread by stretching it; if it breaks, it won't do for wheat weaving.

~ Window screen, for drying projects

~ Sheet of cardboard or rigid polystyrene foam, also for drying projects

~ Straight pins, for use in drying projects and for attaching some project parts to others

Additional Tools and Supplies

~ Large-eyed upholstery or tapestry needles, for stitching together the sections of some projects

~ Clothespins, which can take the place of fingers when you don't have enough of the latter to go around

~ Craft knife, for splitting straws and removing pith from them

~ Splitter, also for splitting straws. A ribbon shredder, available at paper and ribbon-supply companies, will give similar results.

~ Crochet hook, for opening the ends of splits before ironing them

~ Iron, for flattening split straws

~ White craft glue, for gluing straw splits to a backing material. Widely available, these glues will set and dry thoroughly in about 30 minutes, depending upon the surface material to which the straw is being applied. Craft glue won't last forever, but will hold for about 20 years.

~ Burnishing tool, for ensuring strong glue bonds in appliqué work. Shown in the photo on page 21, this tool is commonly used in the graphics-art industry. After you spread glue onto one surface of a straw split and press the split into place, you'll rub its exposed surface with the rounded tine of the burnisher in order to spread the glue evenly underneath the split.

Your Hands

Your hands are your most important tools, so do make an effort to protect them and use them properly. The tips that follow will help both your weaving and your physical health:

~ If you're tense as you weave, your hands will be likely to tighten their grip. Relax and let the wheat do the work. A tight grip won't improve the weave, may dry out the straws prematurely, and can cause hand cramps.

~ Repetitive hand motions can cause carpal tunnel syndrome. Avoid working on the same type of braid for longer than 90 minutes at a time. Change the style of weaves you create in any given braiding session and take frequent breaks.

~ Make sure that your chair provides good back and arm support.

~ Rest your elbows on the table instead of supporting the weave in midair. Avoid resting your forearms on the sharp corners of the work surface.

~ Avoid weaving in cold, drafty areas such as those close to air-conditioning vents.

~ Do a few warm-up exercises before you begin. Make loosely-clenched fists with both hands; then open them up and extend your fingers. Repeat five times for each hand. Slowly rotate your relaxed wrists in circles. Repeat at least three times. Extend your fingers fully; then bring them, one-by-one to your palm, working from your little finger to your thumb. Repeat six times. Stretching your entire body is also relaxing and will help make your weaving more successful.

Learning Hand Positions for Wheat Weaving

Certain hand positions (we'll refer to these as HPs) make particular weaves easier to accomplish. The six suggested positions described and illustrated in this section prove comfortable for many wheat weavers, but if they aren't comfortable for you, by all means use any that are. (Keep in mind that the illustrations in this section show only how to hold the straws and where the heads and finished plaits should fall. They don't demonstrate how specific plaits are woven or how many straws to use.)

No matter which hand position you're using, maintaining the correct straw angles is always easiest when you hold and work the straws as close as possible to the portion of the plait that has already been completed.

HP #1

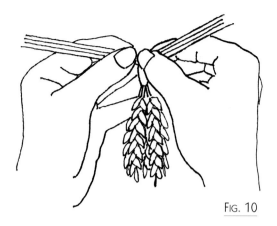

Fig. 10

This hand position (Fig. 10) is used to support the straw between the first two fingers and thumb of your nondominant hand (whether right or left). The other hand controls the movement of the straws. Note that in this position, the finished braid and the wheat heads are below your hands. For braids that require repeating a series of moves on the left and then on the right, just alternate using your nondominant and dominant hands to hold the plait.

HP #2

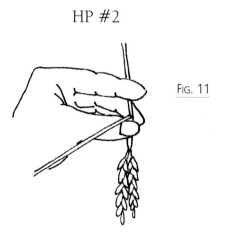

Fig. 11

HP #2 is used to make plaits in which the straws are pulled down perpendicular to the heads. (The plait will develop below your hands.) Hold the straws between the middle finger and thumb of your nondominant hand, using them as adjustable "tables" on which to position the straws at specific angles (Fig. 11). Tilt your hand away from you, at an angle of about 45 degrees. Use the index finger of the same hand to help hold down the straws in position as you work.

HP #3

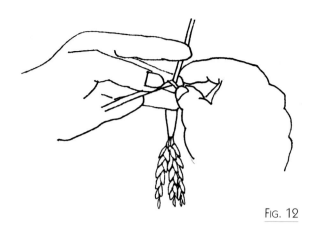

Fig. 12

This position (Fig. 12) will enable you to maintain tension on the straws. Hold your palm at a 45-degree angle and cradle the straws between your middle and third fingers. Your thumb and index finger will be free to hold the straws in position.

HP #4

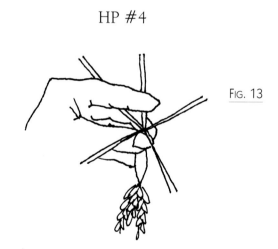

Fig. 13

Position #4 (Fig. 13), which is similar to HP #2, is used to make tubular plaits in which the straws are moved in a circular pattern. Support the straws between your middle finger and thumb, but rather than tilting your hand away from you, hold it vertically and somewhat higher than in HP #2. By using your index finger to hold the working straw (the straw that has just been "worked" around the plait) in place, you'll secure the rest of the straw positions in the plait.

HP #5

FIG. 14

An alternative to HP #4, this position is one in which the length of the plait is supported between the middle and third fingers, with the palm held face up and not at an angle, but flat (Fig. 14). Use the thumb of the same hand to hold the straws down on your palm while you work the plait with your other hand.

HP #6

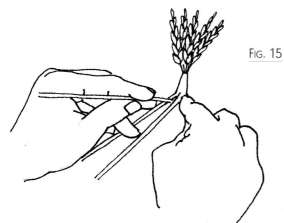

FIG. 15

You'll use HP #6 to make many of the flat Ribbon plaits. Place the straws on the work surface, with their heads facing away from you, and work the weave toward you by lifting the straws with the index finger and thumb of each hand, using your other fingers to push straws to the opposite side (Fig. 15). Further instructions on this position are provided in the "Ribbon Plaits" section of Chapter Three.

Preparing Yourself for Wheat Weaving

Successful wheat weaving involves three things. One is good technique. The ability to manipulate a particular braid or plait well is always something to strive for—and will come with practice. The second is careful construction. Attaching and tying into place the various parts of a project should be done accurately and efficiently. As you learn construction methods, keep the following tips in mind:

~ Don't stint on thread when you cut lengths for knot-tying, but avoid using a lot of thread to make the actual knot. A tight and accurate tie will work better than wrapping a lot of thread around your work.

~ Sometimes you'll need to tie one part of a project to another part that has also been tied with thread. When you do this, place the new tie on top of the old one. A tie that is placed just a fraction of an inch beyond another tie won't look attractive.

—Rather than clumping wheat heads together, fan them out to display them.

The third component of success is you and your imagination. Even a technically perfect project can be improved when you add your own special flare to it. Whether you become an expert wheat weaver or remain an enthusiastic hobbyist, the process should always be enjoyable, and you should always feel free to add distinctively personal touches to your work. Your choice of materials, a turn of the straw, an additional wheat head draped across the center of a design—these and other special touches can personalize even a traditional design—and should.

3

Making the Basic Plaits

I n this chapter are instructions for making a number of basic *plaits* (also called braids or weaves). Any one of these can be displayed as an attractive project, but many also appear within the more sophisticated projects in Chapters Four through Eight. We've designated the latter plaits with a Be sure to practice weaving them, or you'll be limited in your selection of projects later!

Learn the plaits in sequence, practice each one until you feel confident, and then move on to the next. If you skip around, you may miss a technique required in a more complex plait. Don't let the difficulty of any given braid stop you from progressing, however. If you have trouble understanding a particular braid, move on to the next, as it may make previous ones clearer.

Starting Tips

~ Avoid using your highest-quality or longest straws when you're practicing. Save these for your finest work!

~ Remember to soak your straws before you start.

~ Select straws of equal diameter for any given braid.

~ When you tie straws together to start a braid, always tie them just below their necks.

~ To make sure you get enough practice as you work, weave at least one complete plait, manipulating the straws until you've woven them to their ends. (Instructions for making longer plaits by adding new straws are provided in specific sections.)

~ Most plaits are finished off by tying the straws together at their ends. Be careful to tie the straws evenly, or the end of the plait may look misshapen.

~ With apologies to "lefties," we'd like to point out that most of the text and illustrations in this book have been designed for right-handed weavers. If you're not right-handed, just use opposite hands to achieve the same effects.

~ To finish any of these plaits, be sure to dry them as described on page 22.

~ Which surface of a finished plait should you display—the one that faced you as you worked the plait or the opposite side? This won't be an issue with tubular plaits, of course, or with any plait the two surfaces of which are identical. For plaits with two different surfaces, however, the list that follows offers recommendations as to which will look best. (Rules exist to be broken, of course; many weavers select the surface that strikes their fancy.) The plaits that aren't listed will look fine no matter which surface shows.

Display Working Surface

Luton Railroad

Catfoot

Thirteen-Straw Fancy

Raised Diamond

Chinese Chain Rickrack

Display Non-Working Surface

Five-Straw Ribbon

Seven-Straw Ribbon

Twilled Ribbon

Rustics

Batwings

The Hair Braids

The braids in this category are among the easiest to weave and are often the first to be taught. Their simple patterns and textures, along with their ease of construction, has made them favorites for centuries.

~ Three-Straw Hair Braid

Tie together three straws. Using HP #1, hold the straws just below the knotted thread and open them up as shown in Figure 1, with two straws at the right. With your dominant hand, move the straw at the right over the straw next to it, to rest just inside the straw on the left. Then move the left-hand straw over the middle straw until it lies just inside the one on the right (Fig. 2). Repeat by continuing to move the working straw over the middle one to lie just inside the straw on the opposite side (Fig. 3).

Tips

~ Keep the straws at right angles to each other. If the angle begins to close up into a shallow V-shape, the look of your braid will be affected adversely.

~ Hold the braid just under the portion being worked and move your hand up the plait as it lengthens.

~ Two variations will give this braid more volume and texture. To make the first of these, shown in the photo above, tie together six straws. Using HP #1, manipulate the straws in pairs, moving two straws instead of one with each manipulation (Fig. 4). To give the braid more texture, make the straws in each pair rest on top of each other by pulling each pair tightly as you move it.

To make a wider braid with an interesting pattern, tie together six straws, positioning the three pairs as before, but don't pull them tightly as you manipulate them. Instead, allow them to bend over the middle pair so that they rest side by side rather than on top of each other (Fig. 5). As you continue, you'll see a flat pattern emerge.

When making either of these variations, always hold the middle pair of straws stationary as you bring the other pairs across it.

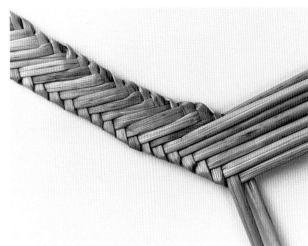

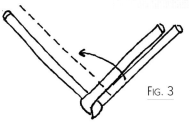

FIG. 3

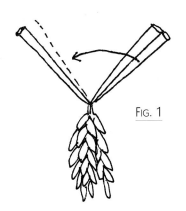

FIG. 1

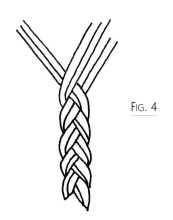

FIG. 4

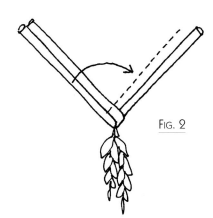

FIG. 2

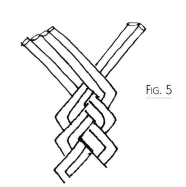

FIG. 5

Luton Railroad

An interesting variation in the Hair-Braid family, this plait is made by positioning a large number of straws on one side and fewer on the other to create an interesting texture and characteristic angle to the weave.

Tie nine straws together. Using HP #1, divide them into two groups, placing seven straws to the right and two to the left, with the two groups at right angles to each other. Locate the second straw in from the outside of the right-hand group. Lift this straw at an angle of about 35 degrees. Bring the outermost straw in this group under the lifted one and over the others, to rest inside the left-hand group (Fig. 6). Return the lifted straw, which now becomes the

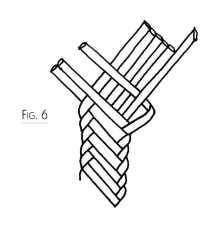

FIG. 6

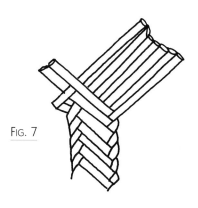

FIG. 7

new outside straw, to its original flat position. The process you've just completed is known as *locking the straws*.

The left-hand group now has three straws. Lift up the outermost straw of this group and pass it over the middle straw and under the inner straw of this group (Fig. 7). Lower the raised straw back into position. Repeat these manipulations, locking first one side and then the other.

Tips

~ When using Luton Railroad plaits in a symmetrically divided project that has two opposing Luton Railroad sections in it, weave the first plait as usual, but start the second plait with seven straws on the left and two on the right and begin locking this plait on the left.

~ To help make the braid's edges visually crisp, create a sharp fold in the outermost straw by giving it a slight turn inward as you move it. This in turn will help keep the front and back surfaces of the plait flat. Also remember that the bend you make should bring the straw to rest parallel and next to the edge of the one next to it.

~ To keep the plait from sliding on a slick work surface, either work it on top of a damp towel or use one hand to move the working straw while pressing the braid down onto the table with the index finger of your other hand. Both methods will work, but a damp towel will also keep your straws moist and pliable.

Fill-the-Gap (or Closed Link) Plaits

Fill-the-Gap (which we'll refer to as FTG) plaits are tubular in shape and appear in many traditional projects worldwide. They're a great deal of fun to weave and, considering the number of straws involved, can be made surprisingly quickly, too.

✎ Four-Straw Fill-the-Gap

You may use either HP #4 or HP #5 to make this plait. HP #5, in which the palm of your hand serves as a table, is especially effective when working plaits that require precise angles, but some people find this position uncomfortable. HP #4 makes a good alternative.

Tie together four straws. Then bend them down so that they rest flat on your palm, perpendicular to the heads below, spacing them as shown in Figure 8. Note the gap, designated by the dotted lines in this figure. Each time you

fill this gap with a straw, you'll create a new gap, which in turn will be filled by the next straw you move.

Move straw A clockwise over straw B and into the gap (Fig. 8). Then move straw C over straw D to fill the gap left by straw A (Fig. 9). Next, move straw B

over straw A to fill the gap left by straw C (Fig. 10). Finally, move straw D over straw C. What you've been doing is moving a straw to fill a gap and then moving the next straw clockwise to the one you just moved. By moving every straw once, you've *set the round*—made a series of manipulations that are repeated until the plait is finished.

Tips

~ Hold the plait securely as you work to make sure the woven straws don't loosen.

~ This plait can be used as is or, as shown in the photo below, stretched to increase its length and change its appearance.

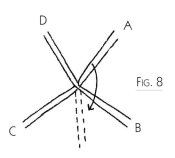

FIG. 8

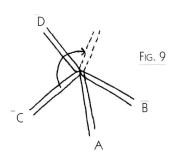

FIG. 9

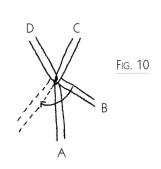

FIG. 10

~ Holding the straws at the correct angles is very important. If, like many beginners, you tend to position the straws at right angles instead, you'll find that they won't overlap each other correctly because they'll end up resting in the same plane. Take a look at the developing braid from one side. The uppermost straw should be the one you just moved, and the bottom one should be the next to be moved.

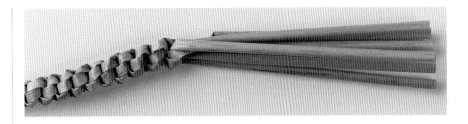

~ Six-Straw Fill-the-Gap

This expanded but easy version of an FTG plait is heavily textured and thicker than the four-straw version but is built in the same manner. (The top straw is the one that has just been moved and the bottom is the next to be moved.) Keep in mind that you must set the round (work every straw once) before you'll have six different levels of straws.

Tie together six straws. Pull them down perpendicular to the heads, spacing them equidistant from one another and then widening the space between straws C and D to create the gap.

Using either HP #4 or HP #5 and referring to Figure 11, move straw A over B and C to rest between straws C and D. Note that the next straw clockwise from straw A is now straw D. Move straw D over E and F to rest between F and B (Fig. 12). Continue by moving the next straw clockwise to straw D, which is straw B, clockwise over two straws. Repeat these moves to continue building your plait.

Tips

~ The Six-Straw FTG may also be used as is or stretched, as shown in the photo at right.

~ Remember to keep tension on the straws as you move them.

FIG. 11

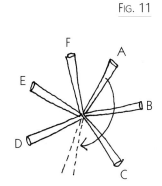

FIG. 12

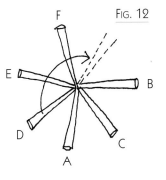

Seven-Straw Fill-the-Gap

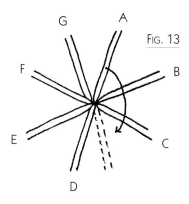

FIG. 13

The Seven-Straw FTG is one of the prettiest of the tubular weaves and appears in many designs, both traditional and contemporary. You may use either HP #4 or HP #5, but you're likely to find the latter more convenient when working with this many straws.

Tie together seven straws. Pull them down perpendicular to the heads as shown in Figure 13, leaving one position empty to form a gap. Move straw A over B and C, to rest in the gap. Skip straw D and move E clockwise over F and G, to rest in the gap left by A (Fig. 14). Skip B (the next straw clockwise from E) and move the next straw (C) clockwise over two straws (Fig. 15).

The manipulation for this FTG is as follows: Move a straw over two straws and into the gap. Skip the next straw clockwise from the straw you just moved and move the second one over two straws into the gap left by the first straw.

Tips

~ Due to the tension in this plait and the number of straws involved, the Seven-Straw FTG is not often stretched. Some wheat weavers roll the plait under a book to give it a nice round look.

~ If you've positioned the straws at the correct angles, after you've set the first round, you'll be able to see that the top straw has created the space or gap and that the bottom straw is the next to be moved.

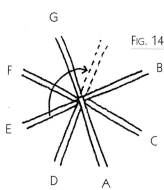

FIG. 14

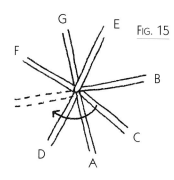

FIG. 15

Compass Weave (Four Straws at Four Corners) Plaits

The Compass Weave and its variations are named for the directions of the straw manipulations required to make them—north, south, east, and west. Excellent all-around plaits with many applications, their characteristic angular corners make them especially useful as borders or bases to which other plaits may be added.

Basic Compass Weave

Tie together four matched straws. Pull them down perpendicular to the heads, spacing them at right angles. Using either HP #4 or HP #5, move straw A up and over to rest next to B and then move B down to the side A was on (Fig. 16). Repeat this manipulation with C and D (Fig. 17). Continue by folding two straws to opposite sides each time.

The straws in each pair should cross over only the straws in the other pair—never each other—or they won't create the corners that distinguish this braid. As you continue to plait, make sure that each straw in a pair stays on the same side (left or right) of its partner.

Tips

~ Turning the plait a quarter-turn clockwise after folding each pair of straws may help you keep track of the repetitions.

~ When you move a straw to the opposite side, pull on it gently to maintain tension so that the fold of the straw is tight.

~ The lower portion of any straw is larger in diameter and coarser in texture than the portion closer to its neck, so your plait will become thicker and coarser as you create more of it. Initially, you'll find that it's easier to manipulate the straws as they thicken; plaiting will be easier after the first several rounds. As the straws grow even thicker and coarser, however, they'll be more difficult to work. In selecting projects and the straws to use for them, keep in mind that the last third of the straw will be coarsest and that you may need to stop weaving at a particular point. When no specific plait measurements are provided with a project, select straws carefully so that you'll have enough length to manipulate.

~ If you're making a project that calls for this braid without the wheat heads attached, tie the four straws together with the thicker ends of two next to the thinner ends of the other two so that the plait will be more even in thickness.

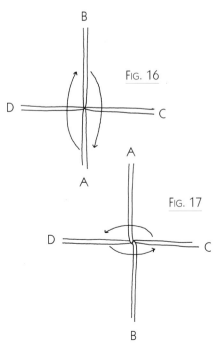

To make this version of the Compass Weave, use HP #4 or HP #5 to move four pairs of straws as if each pair were a single straw (Figs. 18, 19, and 20). Hold the straws in each pair side by side. If they're allowed to bunch up, your braid will have a less precise look to it.

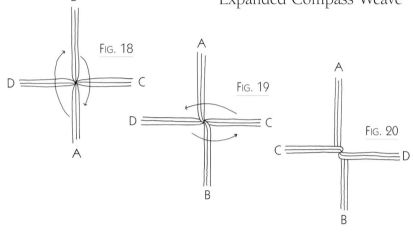

Expanded Compass Weave

Although braids can be gently curved by pinning them onto a drying board when they're still damp, the best way to create and maintain acute angles is to include a wire core in the braid. (Cores are sometimes used to create bulk as well.) The wire core in this braid is hidden within a straw.

Insert a piece of 20-gauge wire into a hollow straw. Then tie four straws, spaced evenly, at one end of it. Using HP #4 or HP #5, pull the four straws down and perpendicular to the straw-covered wire, as shown in Figure 21. (The straw-covered wire should extend above the straws.)

This variation is manipulated in the same manner as the Basic Compass Weave, except that the wire runs up through the center of the braid. As you work around the wire, be sure not to cross a straw to the wrong side of it.

Tips

~ Select a wire gauge to suit your purpose. Twenty-gauge wire—a fine-gauge wire—bends easily, and although it will work for this simple braid, in some projects it may not be strong enough to

Compass Weave with Core

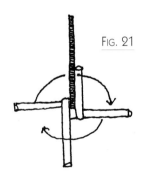

hold the desired shape. For these, use a heavier 16-gauge wire instead.

~ The wire you use must be small enough to fit into the straw without splitting it and large enough to fit snugly. To adjust straws for wires that are too thick to be inserted fully, cut off portions from the narrow end of the straw until the wire will fit all the way in.

Rope Weave

The Rope Weave is very popular because it's quick and easy to make, has a wonderful texture, and can be substituted for other tubular plaits in most designs. In addition, it can be made with straws that aren't top-quality.

To make the Rope Weave, you'll either need to ask someone to hold the heads while you twist and pull the plait to its conclusion or take the time to build a tension-maintaining device to serve the same purpose. This device isn't difficult to build. Glue and nail together two pieces of 1" x 2-1/2" x 6" (2.5 x 6.4 x 15.2 cm) wood at right angles (Fig. 22). Cut one or more notches into the edge of the vertical piece, gauging their widths to match those of the Ropes you might create. Secure the device to your work surface with a C-clamp.

Tie several pieces of straw together. (Try 12 this time; when you're making a project, you'll use as many straws as necessary to give you the desired thickness.) Slip the necks of the straws into the notch of your wooden device, with the heads facing away from you. Divide the straws in half by volume rather than number, so that each group is equal in girth, and place one group to the right and the other to the left.

Using the special hand positions shown in Figure 23, hold the right-hand group securely within the last three fingers of your right hand. Position your right index finger and thumb around this group so you can use them to help to twist the left-hand group.

With your left hand, twist the left-hand group several times as shown, until the straws are rounded. To keep the Rope from unraveling between twists, hold the straws with the thumb and index finger of your right hand. After twisting about 1" (2.5 cm) of rope, switch the two group's positions by passing the twisted left-hand group under the right-hand group. Repeat by twisting some of the new left-hand group and then switching the groups' positions again. Continue until the plait is as long as you like, keeping in mind that you'll always twist on the left.

Tips

~ You may twist longer lengths and make several "switches" at once rather than twisting only a short length prior to each switch.

~ This weave can create hand tension, so in any given session, take breaks by making other plaits as well.

~ Donna Hall of Merced, California, has created a long, narrow piece of plywood with a notch or two cut into one end and a ruler attached down its center (Fig. 24). To use this device, she places it flat on a chair and keeps it stable as she weaves by straddling it with her legs (Fig. 25). She uses the ruler to measure the length of the Rope as she makes it.

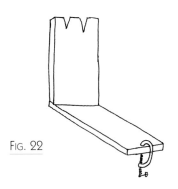

FIG. 22

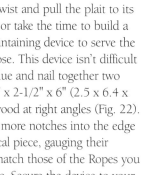

FIG. 24

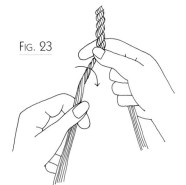

FIG. 23

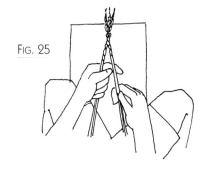

FIG. 25

Catfoot (Three Straws at Three Corners) Plaits

The Catfoot plaits are among the most luxurious of the simple plaits and make fine embellishments. Maintaining the correct angles is extremely important and takes a bit of practice; start by reviewing HP #3, which is the best hand position for this plait.

Basic Catfoot

For a simple three-straw braid, this one is surprisingly wide and textural. Use one of the softer wheats, as the heavier, thicker varieties will be difficult to manipulate.

Tie together three matched straws. Hold them with your nondominant hand, between the middle and third fingers, keeping your palm as flat as possible. Hold the 12 o'clock straw down with the index finger of the same hand, the 8 o'clock with the thumb of that hand, and the 4 o'clock with the thumb of your other hand. You won't be alone if this position feels awkward! Although it's not a good ergonomic hand position, it is one that will facilitate proper stacking of the extreme folds of this plait.

Move the 4 o'clock straw to rest to the right of the 12 o'clock straw (Fig. 26).

Move the 12 o'clock straw to rest in the 4 o'clock position (Fig. 27). Move the 8 o'clock straw to rest to the left of the 12 o'clock straw (Fig. 28). Move the right-hand 12 o'clock straw to rest in the 8 o'clock position (Fig. 29). You've just completed a round of this plait.

Tips

~ Keep the straws from slipping by maintaining a firm grip on the angles of this braid, but don't pinch them too tightly.

~ To prevent excessive hand stress, you may also use a plastic coffee-can lid as a substitute for the palm of your hand. Cut a small hole in the center of the lid, the same diameter as that of your three straws. Manipulate the plait using the same fingers called for in HP #3.

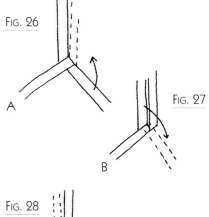

FIG. 26

FIG. 27

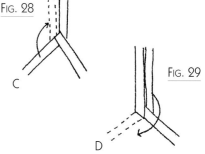

FIG. 28

FIG. 29

Expanded Catfoot

This plait is as beautifully textured as the regular version, but the pattern displayed is wider. The angles of the plait are the same, so the manipulations are very similar.

Tie five straws together so that they rest side by side, holding them flat with the thumb, middle, and third fingers as you tighten the knot. This will make it easier to create the expanded, flat ribbon effect of this braid.

Using HP #3, place two straws at the 12 o'clock position, two at the 4 o'clock, and one at the 8 o'clock. Make sure the straws are perpendicular to the heads and that they rest flat against your palm. Move the upper 4 o'clock straw to the right of the 12 o'clock straw (Fig. 30). Then move the original right-hand 12 o'clock straw (now in

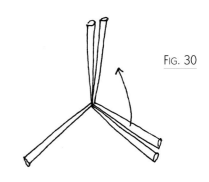

FIG. 30

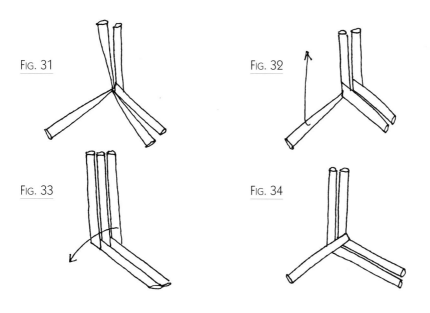

FIG. 31

FIG. 32

FIG. 33

FIG. 34

the middle) to rest above the straw at the 4 o'clock position (Fig. 31).

Repeat this sequence with the two other straws at the 4 and 12 o'clock positions. You have just completed the same movements required to make the Basic Catfoot plait, but you have done so twice.

Now move the 8 o'clock straw up to the left of 12 o'clock (Fig. 32). Move the right-hand 12 o'clock straw over the face of the plait to return to the emptied 8 o'clock position (Figs. 33 and 34). This completes a round. Repeat by beginning again with the upper 4 o'clock straw.

Two-Straw Plaits

Although these plaits are made with only two straws, they're among the most beautiful, graceful, and delicate of all the wheat-woven braids. They can be used as components within projects or as gentle accents to enhance their appearance.

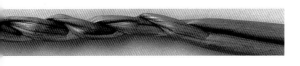

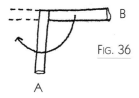 Two Straws at Four Corners

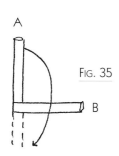

A

FIG. 35

B

B

FIG. 36

A

This important two-straw plait is surprisingly rich in texture. Weaving it is relatively easy, although maintaining the correct tension on the straws takes practice.

Tie together two well-matched straws. Bend them down perpendicular to the heads, positioning them at right angles (Fig. 35). Using HP #2, hold the two straws between the thumb and the middle and third fingers of your nondominant hand. You'll use the index finger of that hand to help hold the straws in place while you manipulate the plait with your other hand. As you weave, move your hand up the plait so that you can maintain the correct angles and prevent the straws from twisting.

This plait is made by moving the straws from one corner to another in an imaginary four-corner box. Start by moving straw A over straw B (Fig. 35). Then move B over A (Fig. 36). By moving each straw to its opposite corner, you've completed a round of this plait. Continue as shown in Figures 37 and 38.

Tips

~ During your first practice session, cut off the head of the wheat and 1" or 2" (2.5 or 5.1 cm) of each straw before tying the straws together so that you can start plaiting with a less delicate section of the straw.

~ To eliminate any twist in the finished, still-damp plait, pull it gently and run your fingers along its edges to release some of the tension in it. Be careful; pulling too hard may loosen the folds in the straw or break the plait.

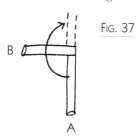

FIG. 37

B

A

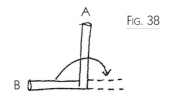

A

FIG. 38

B

This very delicate braid, which is similar in appearance to the Catfoot plait, has a lot of texture and is wide for its size but its angles are less difficult to manipulate.

Tie together two straws and pull them down into a perpendicular plane. Using HP #2, position the straws at two of three imaginary, equally-spaced corners. Move straw A over straw B (Fig. 39). Then move B over A (Fig. 40). Continue to move the two straws in this manner; Figure 41 shows the next move.

▬▬ Two Straws at 120 Degrees (or Two Straws at Three Corners)

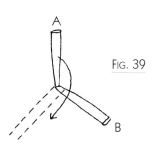

FIG. 39

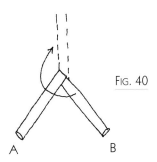

FIG. 40

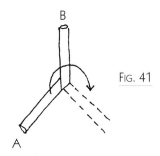

FIG. 41

Arrow and Whip Plaits

Some plaits, including the Arrow and Whip plaits, are woven around themselves or around a core to create a tubular and highly textured exterior surface. These plaits are extremely versatile; they can be used extensively in your own weaving experiments and exchanged with some of the project plaits in this book.

Arrow

The Arrow plait, which is easier to work than some of the plaits you've already learned, is a tubular braid with an unusual pattern and is very useful in projects that require a tubular weave with a core.

First, review the information on cores provided on page 33. You may weave this plait around either a bare wire core or a straw-covered wire core. (If you choose the latter and are making a plait for a specific project, check to see that the straw is long enough for your pattern.) Tie six straws around the base of the core.

Using HP #1, hold onto the straws at the base of the core firmly, but without squeezing. Pull three straws down to the right of the core and three down to the left to form an upside-down T shape. (You'll be building the plait upward around the core.) Because the straws will be bunched together at the base when you start, you'll have to select one on each side to serve as the "bottom" straw; you'll move these bottom straws first. After weaving one full round, identifying the actual bottom, middle, and top straws will be easy.

Move the bottom straw of the right-hand group toward you, over the core, and around behind it, to rest at the top of the original right-hand group (Fig. 42). Then move the bottom straw

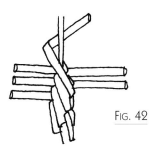

FIG. 42

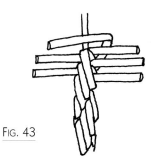

FIG. 43

in the left-hand group away from you, behind the core, and back over its front, to rest at the top of the left-hand group (Fig. 43). You now have new bottom straws in each group. Move the right and left bottom straws as before. You'll have set the first round when you've wrapped all six straws around the core.

Tips

~ The developing plait tends to twist slightly as you move up the wire; don't worry if it does. Traditionally, wheat weavers twist the finished plait to tighten up the pattern anyway.

~ To finish this braid, position the straws parallel to the core and tie them to it.

Four-Straw Whip

Whip plaits, which are tubular weaves with a checkerboard pattern, can be made with different numbers of straws.

Tie four straws together. Using HP #6, divide the straws into two groups of two and either ask a friend to help hold the heads or secure the ends of the wheat in one of the devices described on page 34.

Move the outer right-hand straw away from you, to the left, and behind two straws (Fig. 44). Then bring it forward between the two straws at the left to become the inner straw of the right-hand group (Fig. 45). Continue by moving the outer left-hand straw in the same fashion.

Tips

~ In order to form the tubular shape of this plait, you must maintain tension on the straws as you move them.

~ You may incorporate a bare wire core if you like, weaving the four straws around it, but make sure the wire is thin enough not to be visible when you're finished.

FIG. 44

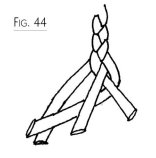

FIG. 45

Eight-Straw Whip

This plait, which must also be secured by a friend or one of the devices described on page 34, is often worked around a core and is similar to the four-straw version.

Using HP #6 and referring to Figure 46, start by moving the outermost right-hand straw away from you, to the left, and around the back of the core. Pull it up between the second and third straws of the left-hand group and over to rest on the inside of the right-hand group (Fig. 47). Repeat, in mirror fashion, with the outermost straw in the left-hand group.

FIG. 46

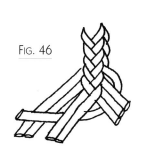

FIG. 47

Ribbon Plaits

Ribbon plaits, which range from simple braids to ones that demand a great deal of practice, were once used to make straw hats and bonnets. Most of these plaits are wide and flat, although some have patterns that give them a raised texture, others are thicker because of the manner in which the straws are manipulated, and still others have raised patterns with distinctive design elements. Descriptions of several basic and intermediate Ribbon plaits follow. Feel free to interchange these plaits in projects.

Use HP #6 unless otherwise specified.

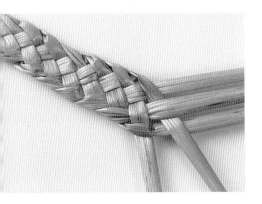

Five-Straw Ribbon

This plait is one of the easiest to make. Tie five straws together side-by-side. Divide them into two groups, spacing the groups at right angles and placing three straws to the right and two to the left. Lift the second straw from the outside (which on this braid is also the middle straw) of the right-hand group slightly. Then pass the outer right-hand straw under it and over the inner right-hand straw to rest at the inside of the left-hand group (Fig. 48). Return the lifted straw to its original position. You have just locked the straws.

The left-hand group now has three straws. Repeat to lock the straws in that group (Fig. 49). Locking the straws on both sides creates a distinctive checkerboard pattern.

Tips

~ When spaces occur between straws in a ribbon plait, beginners tend to overcompensate by pulling the passing straw so tightly that it curls the plait across its width. Spaces are usually a result of incorrect angles or of allowing the straws in a group to spread apart when you pass a straw over them, so to keep your Ribbon plaits wide and flat, pay attention to the angles and keep the straws side by side as you proceed. When you pass the outside straw across, bend it inward to give a nice crisp edge to the plait.

~ Avoid working the straws too far from the center of the braid. As shown in Figure 15 on page 25, you'll have better control of the straws and a better chance of noticing and preventing problems if you work right at the point where the two groups intersect.

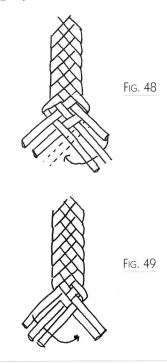

FIG. 48

FIG. 49

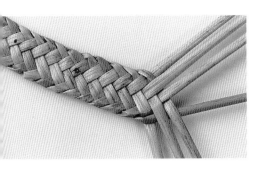

Seven-Straw Ribbon (or Dunstable)

This plait and the five-straw version differ in only two ways. First, as you can see in Figures 50 and 51, the outermost straw in the Dunstable plait passes over more straws in its progress to the other side. Second, you must move two additional straws to complete a round (right straw, left straw, right straw, and left straw in sequence).

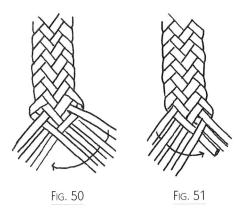

FIG. 50   FIG. 51

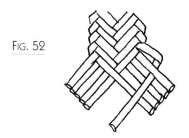

FIG. 52

This plait is created in exactly the same manner as its five- and seven-straw counterparts. The only difference is the wider twilled center that results. To work this plait, use Figures 52 and 53 as guides.

FIG. 53

Twilled Ribbon
(or Eleven-Straw Twilled)

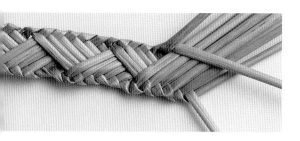

Ten-Straw Diamond

The Diamond plait is an example of a wide, relatively flat Ribbon plait with a raised pattern that makes it thicker than the previous Ribbon plaits you've learned.

Tie together ten matched straws, side by side. Start by spreading five straws to the right and five to the left. Lift up the second straw from the outside of the right-hand group. Pass the outside straw under it and over to the inside of the left-hand group. Return the lifted straw to its original position. Repeat this locking motion until only two straws remain in the right-hand group (Fig. 54).

Switch to the left-hand group and repeat these moves in mirror fashion until all but two straws have been moved to the right-hand group (Fig. 55). As you continue with the next round, the diamond pattern will emerge.

On the last round of this plait, lock back the straws until you have five on each side. Then tie them off to keep the braid from pulling to one side at the end.

FIG. 54

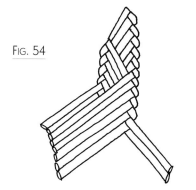

FIG. 55

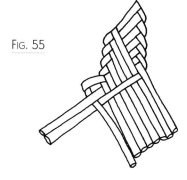

This Victorian plait, once used extensively in the Canadian hat industry, is a beautiful example of how easy it is to create a rich surface texture in a Ribbon plait through a simple manipulation of straws. Historical samples of this plait can be found in the collection of the Parkdale-Mapplewood Community Museum in Lunenburg County, Nova Scotia.

The illustrations for this plait have been drawn for HP #1. You may use HP #6 instead, weaving the plait on a table with the straws facing you, but if you do, the illustrations won't be as helpful. You'd have to flip them over backward to reflect the manipulations accurately.

Tie thirteen straws together, flat and side by side. To accomplish this without letting the straws bunch up, first divide the straws into one group of eight and one group of five. Tie each group separately and then tie the two together. Part the straws into their original groups.

To complete a round, you'll work this plait three times on the right and three times on the left. Start by moving the outermost right-hand straw over the one next to it, under the next two, and over the final four, to rest at the inside of the left-hand group (Fig. 56). Next, move the new outermost right-hand straw over the one next to it, under the next two, and over the last three (Fig. 57). Then move the new outermost right-hand straw over the straw next to it, under the next two, and over the last two (Fig. 58). Eight straws are now on the left and five on the right. Repeat these three steps in mirror fashion by moving three straws from the left-hand group to the right.

Tip

~ When you make Ribbon plaits with this many straws, it can be difficult to keep the straws from shifting positions and to keep track of which one is which. In addition, problems may not

Thirteen-Straw Fancy

become apparent until several rounds have been completed. Going back won't work because bent and creased straws don't weave well, so be very careful to keep the straws in their proper positions. After you become familiar with making these braids, you'll be able to tell when you've manipulated them incorrectly.

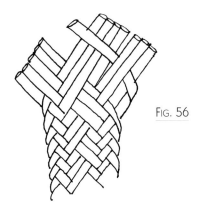

FIG. 56

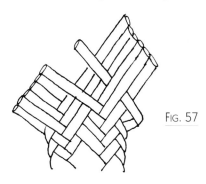

FIG. 57

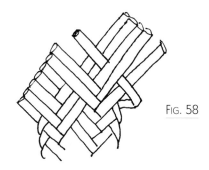

FIG. 58

Its characteristic diamond pattern is this plait's only similarity to the Ten-Straw Diamond. Its more heavily textured pattern, which is created in a very different manner, makes the Raised Diamond quite thick.

Tie together eleven straws, flat and side by side. Divide the straws into one group of nine at the right and one group of two at the left and spread the groups to form a right angle. Lift the

Raised Diamond

second straw from the outside of the right-hand group and pass the outermost straw under it and over the rest in this group (see Fig. 59 on the following page). Remaining on the right are the straw you lifted (now on the outside) and seven straws to its left.

Lift the innermost straw in the right-hand group straight up at a right angle

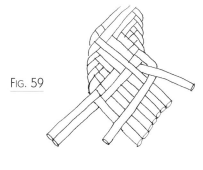

FIG. 59

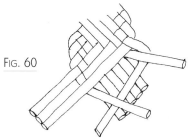

FIG. 60

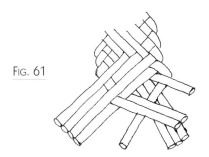

FIG. 61

to the plait, holding it there as you make the next move. Lift the second from the outside straw in the right-hand group slightly and move the outermost right-hand straw under it, over the five flat straws, and beneath the sharply lifted straw, to rest inside the left-hand group (Fig. 60).

Referring to Figure 61, lift up—at a right angle—the next innermost straw in the right-hand group and hold it up with the other sharply lifted straw. Lock once again by lifting the second from the outside straw slightly and bringing the outermost straw under it, over the other straws, and beneath the two sharply lifted straws. Repeat the lifting of another innermost straw and the locking of another outer straw once more (Fig. 62). At this point you should have five straws on the right—two flat and three lifted sharply—and six straws on the left.

Lower the last straw that you raised to a right angle (the one farthest to the right in the right-hand group) back

down to the table to give you three flat straws in that group. Lock the right side by slightly lifting the second straw from the right and passing the outermost straw under it and over the next one. Two flat straws and two sharply lifted straws now remain on the right side (Fig. 63).

Pull down the second straw of those that were lifted up at a sharp angle. Lock on the right as before. Take the last lifted straw, bring it down, and lock as before. You will now have two straws on the right and nine on the left. Make the same sequence of movements with the left-hand group to complete a round.

Tip

~ If you find it difficult to determine which straw is the first, second, or third on the side you're manipulating, study the diamond pattern, and look for the one straw that is at the top and is unsecured by any other straws. This is the third straw on the next side to be manipulated and is the one most often misplaced.

FIG. 62

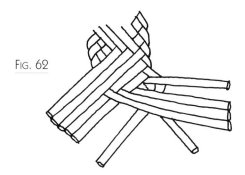

FIG. 63

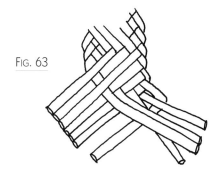

zontal and one vertical. Like all the Tyrolean plaits, this one is worked on the back surface; the pattern shows on the front. Although challenging to learn, it's well worthwhile.

Use HP #1 in order to work this plait in your hand. Tie together four straws and open them up into two pairs to form a narrow V shape, not a right angle (Fig. 64). You'll be moving the bottom straw of each pair over to the other pair and back to the top position in its original group.

Move the outer right-hand straw horizontally over the other right-hand straw and the inner left-hand straw, and under the outer left-hand straw (Fig. 65). Make sure to tuck the base of this working straw all the way down between the two left-hand straws.

To make the vertical manipulation, first bend this same straw forward over both left-hand straws and pinch its base to make a crease in it. Then back it up and move it forward to scissor it under the inner left-hand straw and over to rest at the left of the straw on the right (Fig. 66).

Now repeat these two moves with the outer left-hand straw, first scissoring it horizontally from left to right, over the inner left straw and the inner right-hand straw, and under the outer right-hand straw (Fig. 67), and then moving it vertically over the outer right-hand straw and under the inner right-hand straw to become the inner left-hand straw (Fig. 68).

Tip

~ As with all of your work, make sure you don't allow gaps to appear in the plait. Pull the straws into place if this begins to happen.

Rustic (or Tyrolean)

The Rustic plait is woven differently from most Ribbon plaits; two moves are made with each straw—one hori-

FIG. 64

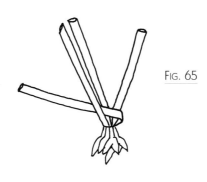

FIG. 65

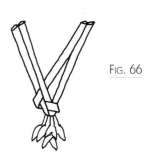

FIG. 66

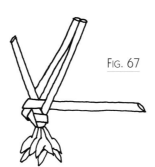

FIG. 67

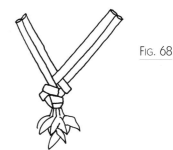

FIG. 68

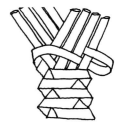

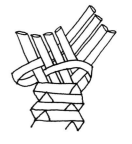

Expanded Rustic

A simple variation of the Rustic, with a twilled pattern in its center that gives it a great deal of character and charm, this plait will help reinforce your understanding of the straw manipulations of this type of braid.

Tie together eight matched straws and open them up into two sets of four straws each. You'll use HP #1 to move the outermost (bottom) straw from one side to the opposite side and then back to the inner (upper) position on the starting side.

Referring to Figure 69, first move the outer right-hand straw horizontally to the left, over all the other straws. Pinch its base to make a crease in it. Then back the straw up and bring it to the left again, over the three inner straws in the left-hand group and under the outermost left-hand straw.

To make the vertical move, first bring this same straw to the right, over the other straws, and pinch its base to make a crease in it. Back it up and then scissor it vertically over the outermost left-hand straw and under the three remaining straws on the left to become the innermost straw in the right-hand group. Repeat this manipulation with the outermost left-hand straw (Fig. 70).

Tips

~ Once the distinctive corners of this plait are made, it's difficult to tighten up the plait, so be careful not to leave any gaps.

~ To create a checkerboard pattern instead, when you make the vertical movement, pass the straw over the outermost straw, under the next straw, over the next, and under the final one to rest in its proper position (Fig. 71).

~ To make a variation that the author has developed, called the Expanded Rustic with Interrupted Twill, tie together twelve straws and separate them into two groups of six straws each. Referring to Figure 72, move the bottom right-hand straw horizontally over to the left, passing it over five left-hand straws and under the outermost left-hand straw. When you move it vertically, pass it back over the outermost straw, under the next four, and over the innermost straw in that group. Repeat on the left to set a round.

Chinese Chain Rickrack

The extra straws added to some Ribbon plaits vary their appearances by creating edging elements. The Chinese Chain plaits include an interesting, elongated edging pattern and are therefore excellent for use as decorative features. The version described here makes use of two "discarded" straws to form a chain that gives the braid a symmetrical, open, lacy look.

Tie five matched straws side by side. Using HP #1 and referring to Figure 73, pull down straws #1 and #5 at right angles to the heads. These are the discarded straws that will form the chain on each side. Straw #2 remains at the center of the braid and is never moved; you'll move the other straws from one side to the other around it. To help you keep track of straw #2, cut it short or mark it.

Start by moving straw #4 over #3 to rest at the right of straw #2 (Fig. 74). Bring straw #5 behind #3; then fold it at a right angle and move it over straw #4 and under straw #2 (Fig. 75). Next, fold straw #4 over straw #2, to rest above straw #5 (Fig. 76). Note that the tension of the straws will pull straw #3 down to the position from which you moved straw #5. You should now have three straws to the left of straw #2 and one to its right.

Now you must work the left-hand straws in the same fashion, while straw #2 remains stationary. Start by moving straw #5 over #4 to rest at the left of #2 (Fig. 77). Bring straw #1 behind #4; then fold it at a right angle and move it over #5 and under #2 (Fig. 78). Finally, fold straw #5 over #2 to rest above #1 (Fig. 79).

To start the next round, mentally renumber the straws from left to right (1, 2, 3, 4, and 5) and repeat these instructions.

Tips

~ When making the 90-degree fold that brings the chain straw to the opposite side, make sure you pull the straw to close any gaps.

~ To help determine whether you're introducing the chain straws at the right time, keep an eye on the edges of the developing chain. If the length between rounds of the introduction of the chain are too long or too short, chances are you've moved the straws improperly. Keep in mind that the straws get thicker as you work farther from the necks and that the spacing will therefore increase a certain amount as a result.

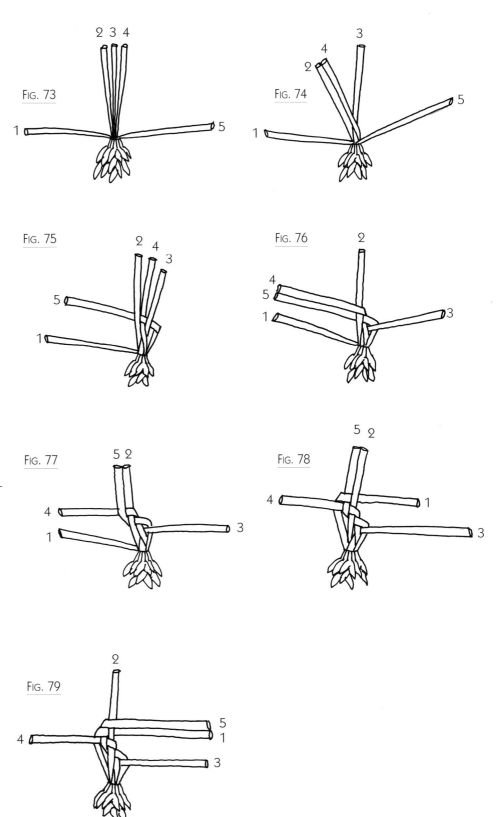

FIG. 73

FIG. 74

FIG. 75

FIG. 76

FIG. 77

FIG. 78

FIG. 79

Edging Plaits

Although there are many types of edging plaits in traditional wheat weaving, this section covers only two of the least laborious and most practical.

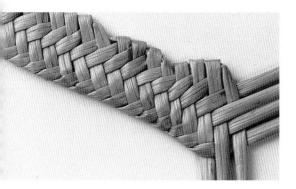

Three-Purl

The scalloped edge of this plait is made by wrapping successive straws around the outermost straw.

Tie seven matched straws together near the heads, placing four straws to the left and three to the right, with the groups forming a right angle. Using HP #1, start the first purl by moving the straw that is the second from the outside in the left-hand group under the outermost straw in this group (Fig. 80) and back over this straw to continue under the two inner left-hand straws (Fig. 81). Bring it to rest at the inside of the right-hand group. Fold the outermost straw in the right-hand group over the right-hand straw next to it and under the two inner right-hand straws (Fig. 82).

To make the second of three purls, repeat the first two steps to manipulate the second-from-the-outside straw in the left-hand group as before and then lock on the right again (Fig. 83). To make the third (and last) purl on the left, repeat again (Fig. 84), locking on the right as well. Then, to close the scallop on the left edge, move the outermost left-hand straw over the one next to it and under the two other left-hand straws (Fig. 85). To complete a round, lock back from right to left as you did before, positioning the straws for a new scallop.

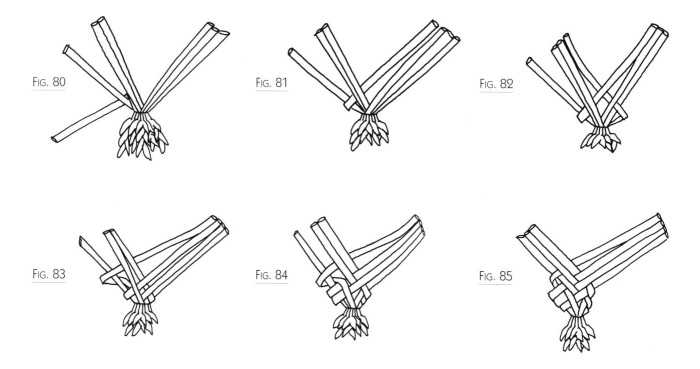

FIG. 80

FIG. 81

FIG. 82

FIG. 83

FIG. 84

FIG. 85

This plait is characterized by the points (called *batwings*) along one of its edges. When you turn the plait over, this edging feature—created by wrapping straws around the outer straw—will appear on the left-hand side of the plait.

Tie nine straws together side by side. Using HP #1, spread six straws to the right and three to the left. Count inward from the right to locate the fourth straw in the right-hand group. Using Figure 86 as a guide, lower this straw underneath the others, wrapping it around to the right. Then bring it up over the three outer right-hand straws and move it under the two inner right-hand straws, to rest at the inside of the left-hand group.

Lock back from the left by moving the outermost left-hand straw over the straw next to it and under the remaining two straws in the left-hand group, to rest at the inside of the right-hand group (Fig. 87).

Using Figure 88 as a guide, count inward to locate the third straw in the right-hand group. Lower this straw under the straws to the right of it, bend it to the right, and bring it up over the three outer right-hand straws and under the two inner right-hand straws, to rest at the inside of the left-hand group. Lock back from the left as before, by moving the outermost left-hand straw over the straw next to it and under the other two straws in the left-hand group, to rest at the inside of the right-hand group.

Now locate the second straw from the outside of the right-hand group. Lower it as before, bringing it up and over three straws and under two (Fig. 89). Lock back from the left once again.

To create the point of the first batwing, use your thumbnail to make a crease in the outermost straw in the right-hand group (Fig. 90). Then pass this straw to the left as before (Fig. 91).

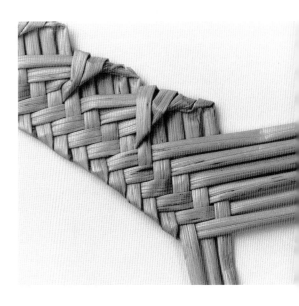

Batwing

Lock back on the left once more, and you're ready to create a new batwing. Start the next round with the fourth straw from the outside of the right-hand group.

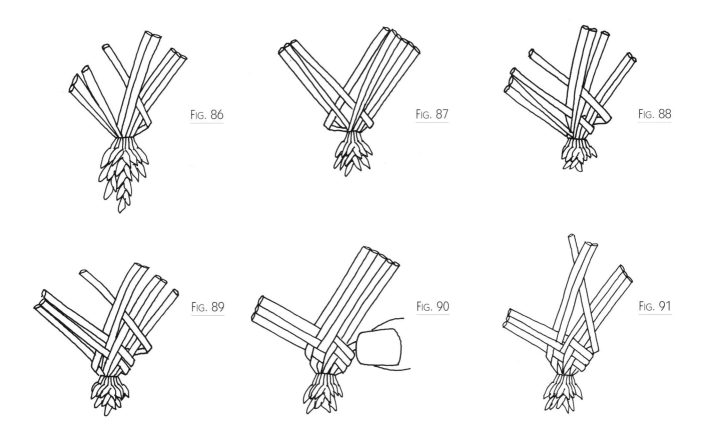

FIG. 86

FIG. 87

FIG. 88

FIG. 89

FIG. 90

FIG. 91

Spiral Weaves

Nothing is more typical of wheat weaving's versatility or range of textures than Spiral weaves, which can vary greatly in width and size and are found worldwide. In addition, inserting new straws into Spirals is very easy, making it possible to create weaves of limitless length. Spirals serve many design purposes, from making arms for Harvest Dolls and legs for rocking horses to creating small figurines and simple borders for straw baskets.

Spirals can be created around either a temporary core such as a pencil (a technique useful for practice sessions) or a permanent core of bunched straws into which a wire is sometimes inserted in order to maintain a specific shape. Some projects don't require cores, but use a pencil core when you practice this weave, as the core will make it easier to see what you're doing.

To visualize a Spiral plait-in-progress, imagine an upside-down umbrella. Its handle represents the core of the plait, and its spokes represent individual straws that have been tied around the circumference of the core at equal distances from each other. This particular umbrella, however, has one peculiarity—a double spoke at one location, just as all Spiral weaves include one pair of straws among the individual straws spaced around their cores.

Spirals can contain four or more straws. The Five-Straw Spiral, which you'll learn first because it's one of the most commonly used, has one straw in each of three corners and a pair of straws in the fourth corner. A Four-Straw Spiral has one straw in each of two corners and a pair in the third corner.

The weaving technique never varies. The corner with the additional working straw, which is usually situated toward the right-hand side of the body as the Spiral is built, is worked first.

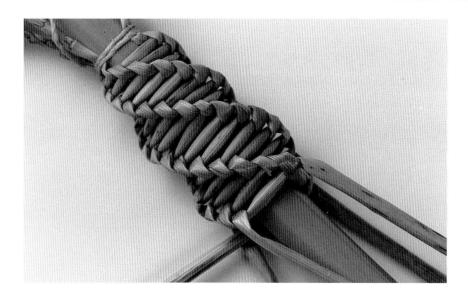

Five-Straw Spiral

Because the four surfaces of this plait are equal in width, if you were to cut across the plait, you'd see a square shape.

Tie five straws at one end of a pencil, spacing them at four equidistant cor-ners, with two straws at one of these corners. Then bend the straws perpendicular to the pencil to form an upside-down umbrella shape.

Start by moving the working straw A (the outer straw in the pair of straws)

clockwise over its mate B, to rest on top of straw C (Fig. 92). Now move straw C over its mate A, to rest on top of straw D (Fig. 93). Move straw D in the same fashion, over its mate C to rest on top of straw E (Fig. 94). Move straw E over its mate D to rest over straw B (Fig. 95). To complete the round, move straw B over its mate E to rest over A. The pattern of movements you've established is as follows: Pass a straw over two straws; pick up the second of the two straws that was passed over; and repeat. Figures 96-99 show this sequence in progress.

Tips

~ Keep the straws straight as you bend them around the pencil. If you pull them too tightly, they'll curve to conform to the pencil shape, and you'll end up with a Spiral the cross-section of which isn't square (Fig. 100). After setting the first round, check for the accuracy of your straw positions. To keep the straws from curving and to make nice, crisp folds, when you move the working straw over its mate to the next corner, hold the mate in place while you bend the working straw against it. If the edges of your Spiral are wide and angular, chances are you're allowing the mate to slip out of position.

~ When using a pencil core to make a Spiral, plait 2" to 3" (5.1 to 7.6 cm) and examine the Spiral to see if it matches your expectations and the instructions. If it doesn't, slide the work off and start over. Practice several times until you can make Spiral corners with regular, even folds.

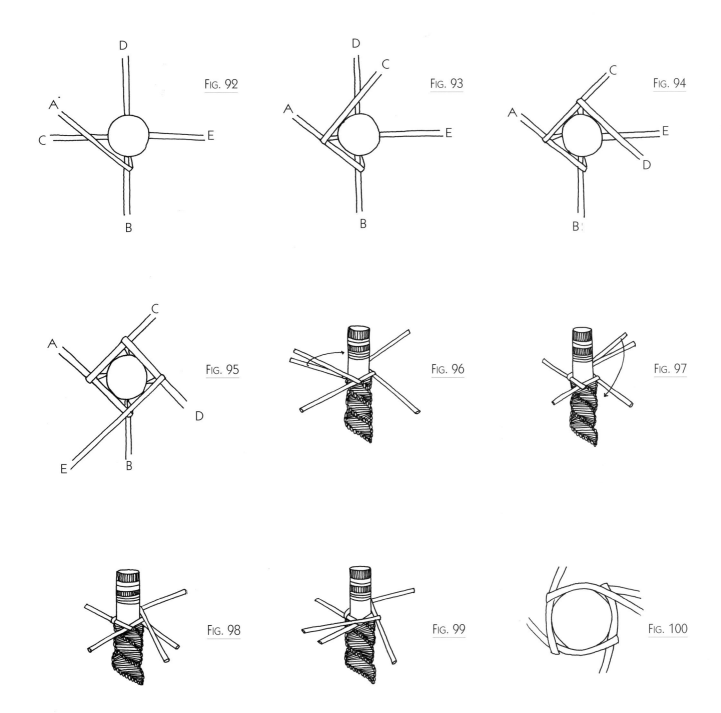

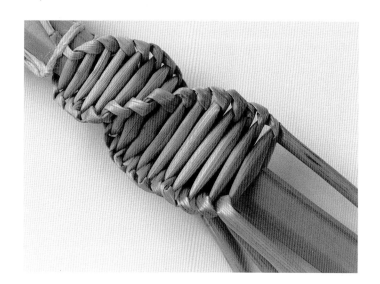

Tie four straws at three equidistant corners around one end of a pencil; one corner should contain two straws. Bend the straws perpendicular to the pencil as before. Move the working straw A clockwise over its mate B to rest on top of C. Then move straw C over A to rest on top of D (Fig. 101). Move straw D over C to rest over B (Fig. 102). To complete the round, move B over D to rest over A. Note that the pattern of movements is exactly the same as those of the Five-Straw Spiral; you're simply working with fewer straws.

Four-Straw Spiral

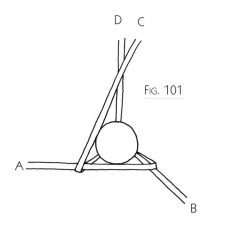

FIG. 101

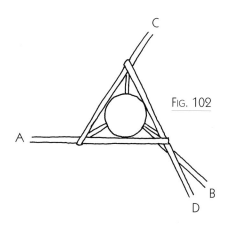

FIG. 102

Six-Straw and Seven-Straw Spirals

These Spirals are made in the same fashion as the others. The Six-Straw Spiral has five evenly-spaced corners and produces a pentagonal cross-section (Fig. 103). The Seven-Straw Spiral has six corners and creates a hexagonal cross-section (Fig. 104). The more straws you use, the more circular the cross-section will look.

Tips

~ Sometimes, you'll want to add new straws to a Spiral: whenever you want to weave a Spiral of any great length; whenever the diameter of one straw becomes thicker than the diameters of the other straws; whenever the texture or appearance of one straw changes in quality; and whenever a straw becomes too thick and coarse to be workable (the straw sections at the ends and just above nodes or leaf joints are too coarse to be pliable even when soaked).

Before you begin weaving, cut the tips of a batch of new straws at angles. The angled ends will fit into the trimmed ends of old straws.

As a rule of thumb, only one new straw should be inserted per round, and the new straw should be inserted just before it will become the working straw, so you must plan ahead. Inserting new straws at the right time will strengthen the Spiral and improve its appearance.

First trim the old straw back with scissors (Fig. 105), using the outer edge of the straw above it as a cutting guide and pressing against the folded straws to hold them back as you make the cut. (These pressed straws will expand back outward to hide the edge of the cut.) Select a new straw the angled end of which is just slightly smaller than the diameter of the hole in the old straw. As you insert the angled end of the new straw into the hole in the old one, support the old straw with a finger so that you don't shove it out of place.

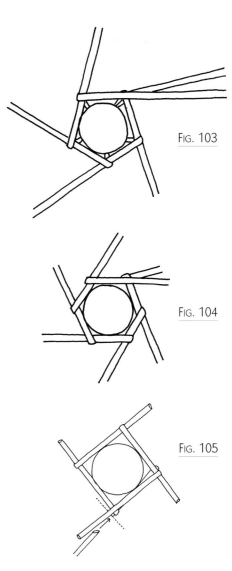

FIG. 103

FIG. 104

FIG. 105

Grouped-Link Plaits

The tubular Grouped-Link plaits have a distinctive texture and can be a lot of fun to create. They're named for the manner in which they're woven: a straw from one group is moved to the next group in order to link the groups.

~ Nine-Straw Grouped-Link

This common Grouped-Link plait is easy to learn and can be incorporated in many projects.

Tie nine straws together and, using HP #4, pull them down perpendicular to the heads, dividing them into four equidistant groups, one with three straws and each of the others with two straws. Position the three-straw corner—your starting point—to the right. Move the lowest straw in this group counter-clockwise to rest at the left of the next group (see Fig. 106 on the following page). Note that straws moved in this fashion help to hold down the straws in the group they join.

Turn your work a quarter-turn clockwise to position the three-straw group to your right. Move the lowest straw in that group as before, to rest at the left of the group above (see Fig. 107). Repeat until all four corners have been worked.

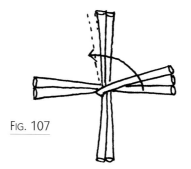

FIG. 106

FIG. 107

~ You'll notice that the folded straws are at right angles and form a square in the center of the plait. Keep your work close and tight. If you begin to see a square-shaped hole developing in the center, you're allowing the lengths to loosen too much and are increasing the width of your braid.

This plait, which the author developed, combines Grouped-Link and Spiral plaiting.

Tie thirteen straws together near the heads around an uncovered, heavy-gauge wire core. Divide the straws into four groups at four corners, three with three straws each and the fourth with four. Because the Spiral develops from bottom to top, try to stack the straws in each group directly above each other. At first, the straw order in each corner will be arbitrary. To start, choose the straw that appears to be the lowest in each section.

As you move around the core from corner to corner, you'll probably think that the number of straws in a particular corner is wrong. Only two straws may be in one corner, while others may have as many as four. The look of this plait is created by moving the straws in an uneven, asymmetrical manner.

Move the lowest straw in the four-straw group A clockwise over group B, to rest on top of the straws in the group C (Fig. 108). Move the lowest straw in group B (the next group clockwise) over group C, to rest on top of the straws in group D (Fig. 109). Repeat this manipulation with a straw from each of the next two corners to set a round of this plait (Figs. 110 and 111).

~ Thirteen-Straw Stacked Spiral Link

Tips

~ Try to keep your groups distinct as you move around the core.

~ Remember that although you're moving straws from one corner to the opposite corner, each straw you move comes from the group adjacent to the last straw you moved.

~ To maintain adequate tension in the braid, pull the straws tightly as you weave.

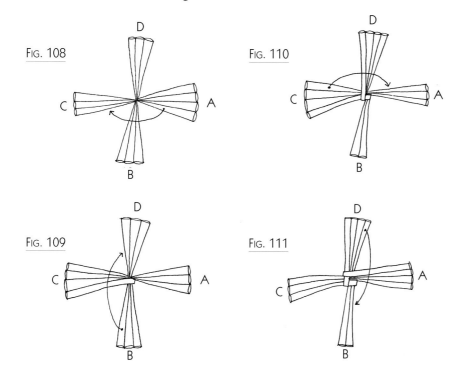

FIG. 108

FIG. 110

FIG. 109

FIG. 111

Moving On

Even the simplest plait, as you've probably discovered by now, has a charm all its own, but once you've learned to make these basic braids, you'll want to move on to even more rewarding designs. In the next few chapters, you'll find three types of projects. Many consist of combinations of plaits you've already learned. Others are new plaits that serve as complete designs within themselves. Still others incorporate these new weaving techniques within more sophisticated designs. The technique used to make the Welsh Fan on page 58, for example, is also used to create the larger Triskeleon design on page 62, and the Corizon on page 64 is used to make the arms of the Shield of the Winds III on page 113.

For Your Browsing Pleasure

Kincardine Maiden
RITA KYSER

Starting Tips

~ Gather your tools and supplies before you begin. If you're not sure which tools you'll need, read the instructions thoroughly before starting.

~ All projects come with lists of the techniques used to make them. Review the pages mentioned in these lists before you start to weave.

~ Although wheat weaving is far from an exact science, the dimensions of a finished project depend to some extent on the size of the wheat used to make each part of it.

Straw length: long, average, and short

Straw diameter: large, average, and small

Head size: large, average, and small

The "Materials" list included with each project may make special recommendations as to wheat dimensions. If none are included, use wheat of average length, diameter, and head size.

As you grow more familiar with the wheat varieties available to you, you'll find that choosing straws of the correct dimensions for a given project becomes second nature.

~ Don't forget to soak your straws before you start!

~ Some plaits are made without tying the straws together first, and some require the addition of new straws as you work. In both these cases, be sure to start weaving at the point on each straw that is just below the neck.

~ Most woven projects are displayed against a wall. To create a hanger, just make a loop with the remaining thread ends left over from a tie or weave a simple braid and stitch its tied ends to the project.

~ To help gauge the skill level and time required to make each project, look for these symbols:

Challenge Rating

Easy

Fairly easy

Moderately easy

Somewhat challenging

Challenging

With a bit of practice and time, even the most challenging projects are well within reach of beginners, so don't feel that if a project looks complex, it's beyond your reach. We recommend brushing up your skills by tackling easier projects first, but if you can't resist tackling a more challenging project right away, don't let us stop you! Just set aside plenty of time, read the instructions carefully, and forgive yourself if you waste a few straws as you work.

Time Rating

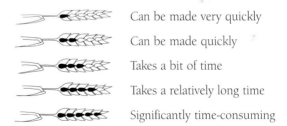

Can be made very quickly

Can be made quickly

Takes a bit of time

Takes a relatively long time

Significantly time-consuming

"Can be made very quickly" will mean one thing to a highly skilled weaver and another to a novice. Once you've made enough projects to estimate your own average speed, however, the "Time Rating" for a given project can help you calculate how long it will take you to make it.

4

House Blessings

House Blessings are probably among the oldest of traditional designs. Each has its own name, but all of them originally shared a single purpose—to provide a home for the wheat spirit after the harvest. Because these straw ornaments were kept until the next planting in the safest place possible—the home—they gradually came to be associated with the safety of the home itself. They were placed near the hearth so the spirit's power could reach the entire household.

Welsh Fan

Welsh Fans are made in almost the same manner as Ribbon plaits, but the straws that are added as the Fan is made open up the simple checkerboard pattern of the Five-Straw Ribbon plait into an ever-widening twilled pattern. The traditional Welsh House Blessing presented here was made with a Plains winter wheat.

Challenge Rating

Time Rating

MATERIALS

25 straws with heads
> Fan

3 straws with heads
> Hanger

TECHNIQUES

Welsh Fan (see this section)

Ribbon plaits (pages 39-45)

Three-Straw Hair Braid (pages 28-29)

The Welsh Fan is always made with an odd number of straws; twenty-five are used in the project presented here. Because so many straws are called for, use HP #6, working the plait on a table with the heads facing away from you. Reviewing the "Ribbon Plaits" section before you start will help you prevent gaps and will ensure crisp edges.

Tie together three straws with heads. Position two to the right and one to the left to create a right angle. The movements you're about to make are as follows: add a straw on the right, add a straw on the left, lock a straw on the right, and lock a straw on the left. Figure 1 shows each of these steps.

Start by adding a straw to the right-hand group, running it under the outer right-hand straw and over the inner right-hand straw, to rest at the inside of the left-hand group. Now add a straw to the left-hand group in the same fashion.

Lock the added straw on the right by lifting the middle straw (or second from the outside straw) and passing the outermost straw under it and over the innermost straw. Then lock the added straw on the left in the same fashion.

Continue to add and lock straws until all 25 have been incorporated (Fig. 2), and then lock, without adding straws, ten additional times on each side, alternating the locks as you make them. Heads that are too large can cause spacing problems. To prevent the heads from bunching up along the Fan's edges instead of resting flat, use smaller bread wheats such as those grown in the Great Plains of the United States. If only larger-headed wheat is available to you, after adding each pair of two new straws, instead of locking once on each side, lock two or three times on each side (alternating the locks from side to side as you make them) before adding the next straws. Doing this will provide the heads with more space in which to flatten out.

To finish off the plait, first turn it 180 degrees so that the straws face away from you. Check to see that there are no gaps in the plait; then tie off each group of straws about 2" (5.1 cm) from the point at which you stopped plaiting (Fig. 3).

Which surface of the Welsh Fan is its front and which is its back? Some wheat weavers (including this author) treat the working surface as the back, so after you've tied off the straws, turn the Fan over before attaching the hanger to the front.

Any basic flat or tubular plait can serve as a looped hanger, but don't choose one with a lot of straws, or the hanger will be too large for the project. To make the hanger shown in the photo, plait three new straws into an 8"-long (20.3 cm) Three-Straw Hair Braid. Tie the end with the wheat heads to the right of the project, with the heads draping downward, and tie the other end to the left. (Be sure to place these ties over the existing ties on the straws.) If you like, you may attach ribbon bows or simple straw embellishments (see pages 136-139) at the same locations.

Tips

~ If your straws differ in size, sort them according to the size of their heads. Work with the largest heads first.

~ When working with exceptionally long straws, turn the heads to face your body so that the straws won't strike you in the chest as you manipulate them from side to side. While this method won't offer the same degree of control over the crisply folded edges of the Fan, it may prove easier for you.

~ Only the straw heads and necks should emanate from the edges of your Welsh Fan; don't let the straw walls protrude.

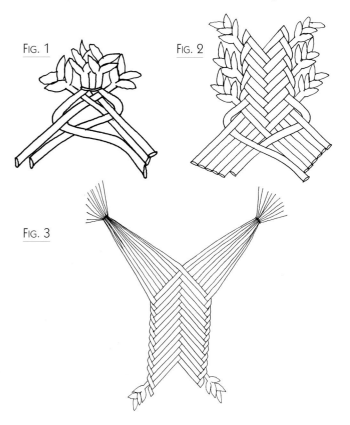

FIG. 1

FIG. 2

FIG. 3

Welsh Harp

Although the project shown here is one of my own designs, wheat-woven harps of different styles have been made for centuries. This more recent design has its roots in many contributions from different wheat weavers and combines a characteristic curved-fan technique with distinctive finishing elements.

Challenge Rating

Time Rating

MATERIALS

19 straws with heads
    Harp

8 long, large-diameter straws without heads
    Strings

TECHNIQUES

Welsh Fan (pages 58-59)

You'll use the Welsh Fan technique to make this project, but because you'll add straws only to the right of your work and not to the left, the woven Fan shape will bend inward towards the left. (As you work, keep in mind that the working surface will be the back of the finished Harp—not the front. Before you display the project, you'll flip it over and turn it 180 degrees.)

To make the main section of the Harp, first tie together three straws with heads. Using the Welsh Fan technique described in the previous section, add a straw on each side and make alternating locks, one on each side. Then add a new straw on the right side, but not on the left. Lock on each side as before (Fig. 4). Make another two sets of alternating locks in order to leave plenty of space for the large heads.

Continue by adding the remaining straws with heads to the right side only and locking three times on each side after each addition. If the additional locks create too much space between the heads, cut back to two locks per straw.

Remember, you're working on the back of the Harp and building it upside down. The wheat heads should be at the top and right at this point. Be careful to maintain the proper tension on the straws so that no gaps occur. If the tension doesn't pull the Fan into a sufficiently deep curve, you may shape the damp straws when you're finished.

After you've added all the straws with heads, lock eight more times on each side, alternating the locks as you make them. Now you must pass the straws in the right-hand group (there should be three of them) over to the left-hand group. To do this, first lock two of them over to the left as usual. Then simply fold the final straw over to the left-hand group; because it stood alone, it won't be locked by another straw. Tie off the straws about 2" (5.1 cm) from the end of the plaited section and trim the straw ends about 1/2" (1.3 cm) from this tie.

To start making the strings of the Harp (the sharply bent straws), first tie together eight straws without heads, flat and side by side and trim them about 1/2" (1.3 cm) above the tie. Then place them parallel to and on top of the tied Fan straws, overlapping the tied ends of each group (Fig. 5). Tie the two groups together, knotting the thread over the previous ties.

To form the sharp angles of the strings, set a ruler across the eight straws, about 2" (5.1 cm) from the tied area, as shown in Figure 6. Crease the straws by lifting their loose ends up against its sharp edge. Pinch each crease to ensure a crisp angle.

Starting with the creased straw that is closest to the starting point of the Fan, bring the loose ends of these eight straws up to the starting point so that each straw overlaps the one beneath it (Fig. 7). Note that the bend in each straw should be slightly lower than the bend in the straw beneath it.

Tie the ends of all eight straws to the Fan's starting point, and trim their ends very close to the knot, taking care not to disturb the straw angles. Display the Harp as shown in the photograph.

Tips

~ You may add embellishments (see pages 136-139) to the base of the Harp if you wish.

~ To help the Harp retain its curve as the straws dry, pin it down onto a sheet of cardboard or rigid polystyrene foam. (Never insert the pins through the straw itself. Use them to brace the edges of the design instead.) The same technique will help flatten any weave that tends to curve due to the tension of the straws.

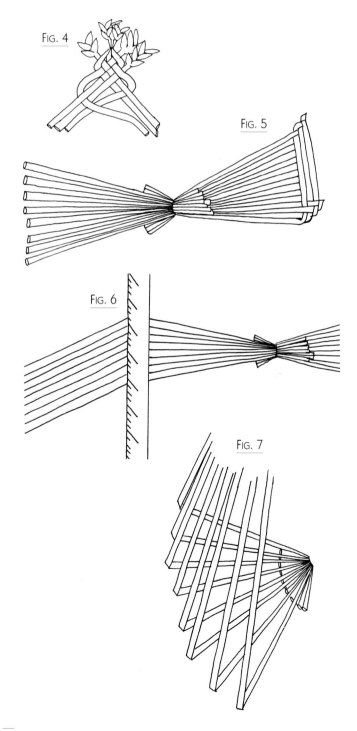

FIG. 4

FIG. 5

FIG. 6

FIG. 7

Triskeleon

Challenge Rating

Time Rating

One of the designs created with the Welsh Fan technique is the Triskeleon—a heraldic symbol thought by farmers to be protective in nature and also considered by many people to be a symbol both of the sun and of manhood. The version presented here was made with black bearded wheat.

MATERIALS

45 long, large-diameter straws with heads
   Legs (three)

6 to 9 straws without heads
   Coil

TECHNIQUES

Welsh Fan (pages 58-59)

Welsh Harp (pages 60-61)

Three-Straw Hair Braid (pages 28-29)

Adding new straws to Hair Braids (see this section)

Straw coil (page 138)

To make one of the three legs, use the Welsh Fan technique to manipulate 15 straws with heads, just as you did to make the Welsh Harp. After all the straws have been added to the right side of the design and locked, lock eight more times on each side. Then, as you did with the Harp, lock the remaining straws in the right-hand group across to the left. Tie off the straws of each Fan about 2" (5.1 cm) from the end of the plait. Repeat to make the other two legs.

As you can see in the photo, the front surfaces of the Fans—not their back surfaces—are displayed in the finished design. To form the Fans into the S-shapes shown in the photo, pull the top of each one sharply toward the right, making an acute bend, as the tension of the straws will tend to lessen this bend as the project dries. In order to preserve their curved shapes, you may find it necessary to pin the Fans before drying.

The large coil in the center of the project is made with a 20"-long (50.8 cm) Three-Straw Hair Braid. Start weaving with one set of three straws. When the middle straw begins to get short, change texture, or get too large in diameter, add a new straw by placing it on top of the old one and continuing to plait (Fig. 8). Because the middle straw is stationary, the first and third straws will secure the new one in place. Tug slightly on the old straws to hold the new straw down until it is manipulated into the plait. (The end of the old and new

straws may protrude from the braid; you'll trim them off later.) Insert two more new straws in the same fashion, and, if necessary, another set of three new straws. Be sure not to insert the new straws too close to each other, as doing so will create a weak spot in the braid. Tie off the braid when it's finished and trim away any protruding straw ends.

To shape the coil, refer to the instructions on page 138. When you're finished, run two or three straight pins horizontally through the body of the coil to keep it from unraveling.

Arrange the three legs as shown in Figure 9 and tie them together securely. Then attach the coil over them by stitching or gluing it to the center.

FIG. 8

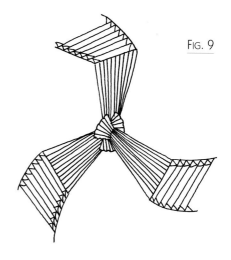

FIG. 9

Corizon

The Corizon is a House Blessing from Mexico, one which some folklorists believe was brought to that country by Moors in the army of Cortez. Its name, which means "heart," may offer a clue as to how native Mexicans viewed this blessing—as the heart of the home. It may also indicate either the placement of the ornament in the house or the nature of its importance to the family.

Challenge Rating

Time Rating

MATERIALS

24 long straws with heads
    Corizon and hanger

TECHNIQUES

Corizon (see this section)

Three-Straw Hair Braid (pages 28-29)

Start by forming an X-shape with two straws, crossing them so that the heads and 1" (2.5 cm) of each straw are above the intersection and the longer portions are below. The head of the upper straw should be at the right and the head of the lower straw at the left.

In this project, straws are always added at the right, beneath other right-hand straws. Using Figure 10 as a guide, place a new piece of wheat just below and next to the right-hand straw. Wrap its lower portion around the left-hand straw and over the right-hand straw to rest above the head of the left-hand straw.

Now pick up the entire weave and turn it over, being careful to hold the woven section so that it doesn't come apart. Referring to Figure 11, add another new straw in the same fashion.

Each of the two straws you've added must be locked into position. To do this, first pull the uppermost right-hand straw down across the left-hand straws (Fig. 12). Turn the Corizon over again and repeat to lock the other new straw (Fig. 13). You have now completed one round. As you continue to add and move straws to the opposite side, you'll be working over an increasingly large base. Try to keep the heads from bunching up, or your straws will crease as you work them.

Repeat these manipulations (add, turn over, add, lock, turn over, and lock) until all 24 straws have been incorporated. You won't be able to lock the last two of these straws, as no new straws will have been added after them. To secure them in place, either tie each one as shown in Figure 14 or tuck the straws under the locks of the previous rounds.

Turn the Corizon 180 degrees so that the heads face you. Using the uppermost three straws on each side, weave two 6"-long (15.2 cm) Three-Straw Hair Braids. When you're finished, tie off each braid and trim the thread ends. Then tie the ends of the braids together to form a hanger.

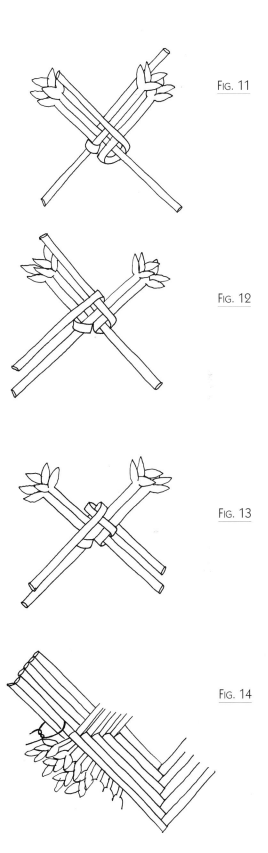

FIG. 11

FIG. 12

FIG. 13

FIG. 14

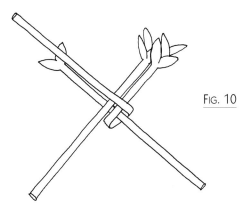

FIG. 10

Mariée de la Moisson

This House Blessing comes from France and includes a Moroccan Fringe, which is a North African weaving technique. I've used a winter Plains wheat, but you may want to add an element of excitement and richness to this old, earthy design by using your most colorful wheat.

MATERIALS

80 long straws with heads
    Entire piece

TECHNIQUES

Moroccan Fringe (see this section)

Challenge Rating

Time Rating

To make the core for this project, tie 20 straws together near the heads. Also tie their ends together loosely to secure them temporarily.

Referring to Figure 15, start by placing five straws perpendicular to and on top of the necks of the core straws, with their heads to the left. Then wrap the five straws around and behind the core and over themselves, bringing the ends to rest at the left of the core. Try to keep the five straws flat and side by side as you pull them around the core and into position.

Now repeat in mirror fashion, placing five more straws with their heads to the right of the core, just below the first set (Fig. 16).

Continue wrapping groups of five straws, first on the left and then on the right, until each side of the core has six groups of straws. Remove the temporary bottom tie from the base of the core and tie all the straws together 1/2" (1.3 cm) below the last wrap (Fig. 17). Trim the straw ends 3" (7.6 cm) from the tie and fan them out before drying.

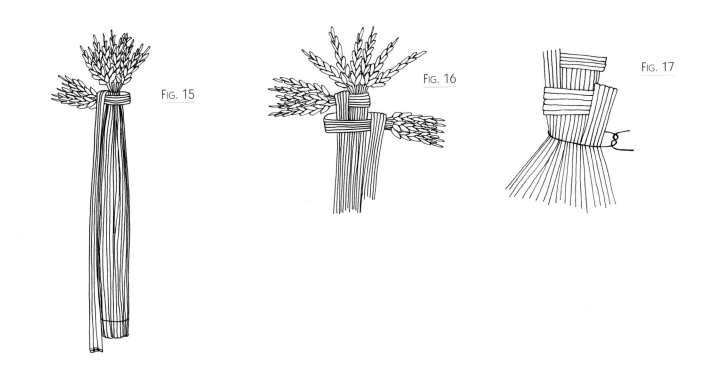

Fig. 15

Fig. 16

Fig. 17

Alchemy

Alchemists of medieval times believed they could turn lead and other base metals into gold. One key ingredient of their concoctions was earth, the symbol for which was a circle with an equilateral cross in the center that represented the division of the earth into four directions, or winds. The Alchemy design, which includes this symbol, was created as a protective charm and is a beautiful example of how traditional techniques—in this case, the Moroccan Fringe—can be used to make larger and more complex designs.

MATERIALS

1 brass hoop, 14" (35.6 cm) in diameter
Braid-covered hoop

27 long straws without heads
Braid-covered hoop

80 long, large-diameter straws with heads
Cores (four)

4 straws without heads, each 8" (20.3 cm) long
Cores (four)

4 pieces of heavy-gauge wire, each 8" long
Cores (four)

200 long, large-diameter straws with heads
Arms (four)

TECHNIQUES

Three-Straw Hair Braid (pages 28-29)

Adding new straws to Hair Braids (page 63)

Straw-covered wires (page 33)

Moroccan Fringe (pages 66-67)

You'll start by making 60" (152.4 cm) of Three-Straw Hair Braid with which to wrap the brass hoop. Tie three long straws together and begin your Hair Braid as usual. In order to complete a braid of the length required, you'll need to insert a full set of three new straws after every several inches of braid, staggering the three straws in each set so as not to weaken the braid.

When the braid is finished, trim the ends of the last set of new straw inserts about 1/2" (1.3 cm) from the braided section. Tie the starting point of the braid to the hoop. Then wrap it around the hoop (Fig. 18), using clothespins spaced at 6" (15.2 cm) intervals to secure the wrapped braid as you work. The visible portions of the hoop should be about the width of the braid itself. Tie the other end of the braid over the starting tie and trim away any straws that protrude.

The four arms of the equilateral cross, with their Moroccan fringe, are modified versions of the Mariée de la Moisson. Each arm consists of a twenty-straw core covered with a total of ten five-straw groups instead of twelve. To make each arm, tie the core straws beneath the heads and follow the Mariée de la Moisson instructions to create arms that measure exactly 5" (12.7 cm) from the starting tie to the ending point. Before you tighten the ending knots, insert an 8"-long (20.3 cm) piece of straw-covered wire into the center of each core, so that a 3" (7.6 cm) length of straw-covered wire extends beyond the ending tie. Then tighten the knot at the bottom to secure both the plait and the wire.

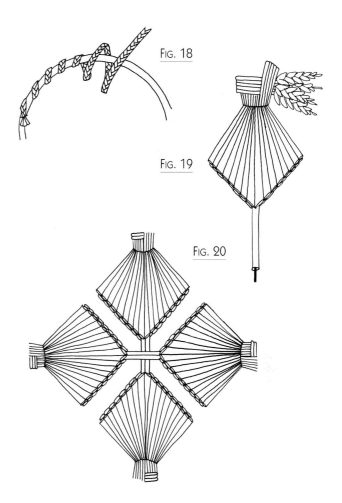

FIG. 18

FIG. 19

FIG. 20

Trim the ends of each arm as shown in Figure 19, locating the pointed base of the V shape exactly 2" (5.1 cm) from the ending tie, to make each arm 7" (17.8 cm) long from its tied starting point to the base of the V. Two inches (5.1 cm) of straw-covered wire should extend beyond the point of the V.

Assembly of this project takes a bit of care. Position one arm underneath the wrapped hoop so that its starting point lies directly underneath the tied ends of the Hair Braid. Tie the arm in place, covering the Hair-Braid ties with your thread. Tie the second arm at a point 180 degrees from the first arm. Now you'll attach the two arms to each other. With the hoop resting flat on your work surface, lift one arm, bend the protruding wire that extends from its end, and insert it into the core of the other arm. Repeat with the opposite arm and lower both arms back onto the work surface, bending the wires straight as you do.

Add the other two arms in the same fashion, positioning them at right angles to the first two. The four wires should intersect at the center of the hoop, as shown in Figure 20. Note that this illustration shows the wires. If you've measured correctly, they won't be visible; the tips of the straws in each arm will cover them. Turn the project over and tie the wires securely at their intersection to strengthen the center of the design.

5

Love Knots
and
Courting Favors

Woven symbols of love—many patterns for which still survive—served as an integral part of rural courting customs, both as a swift means of introduction (Love Knots are easy to make) and as public declarations of one's "tie" to another. Originally, the Love Knot—both the name of a weave and a classification into which many traditional designs fit—was probably a simple Hair Braid that was tied into a loose knot. Worn over a woman's heart, the braid indicated that the wearer was romantically tied to the man who had woven the braid. If a Knot was worn on the right, it suggested that courting would be welcomed. While many Love Knots were simple in design, some were very intricate, and even more elaborate tokens—too large to wear—were made for display in loved ones' homes. Gradually, designs of this type became so popular that they were copied for their tender and romantic appeal. Courting Favors, also symbols of love, were often made as a means of spending time with a loved one (see Chapter One). Gifts filled with symbols of love, Courting Favors could be quite complex, as the weaver hoped that the intricacy of his design might indicate to his sweetheart how much time he spent thinking of her. Sometimes, two lovers worked on a Courting Favor together, getting to know each other—and how well they might or might not work together—in the process. Some folklorists believe that symbols woven into the

together—in the process. Some folklorists believe that symbols woven into the designs represented promises and that the Favors were a form of rural marriage contract. The number of interlocking woven chains in a design, for example, indicated how many children were hoped for in the marriage. Different types of flowers promised faith in love, devotion, or passion.

Both Courting Favors and Love Knots were often displayed on rural wedding altars. In many cases, the weavings were later placed over the bed of the newly married couple in order to promote fertility as well as love. Because many a heart was won with these weavings, the designs were often passed down through the generations. As a result, many wonderful Love Knot patterns have been preserved.

Spiral Castle
Morgyn Geoffry Owens-Celli
The author spent more than 6,000 hours, over a span of five years, designing and constructing this piece, which was completed in 1984 and first exhibited in 1992.
Photo courtesy of photographer Michael G. Patton

Love Knots

All the Love Knots shown in the photograph were made in the same fashion as weavers used hundreds of years ago. When a woman wore one of these delightful plaits over her heart, people knew that her love had been claimed by the weaver.

Challenge Rating

Time Rating

MATERIALS

3 to 7 straws with heads
   Braid (one)

TECHNIQUES

Love Knots (see this section)

FIG. 1

Any favorite plait that contains seven or fewer straws can be transformed into a Love Knot, so select any braid you like. Your choice will give your Love Knot a special look all its own.

Weave 6" to 8" (15.2 to 20.3 cm) of the plait. The more straws called for in your selected plait, the longer the braid should be, as a short, thick braid will make a Knot that's too tight to be attractive.

Tie the plait in a loose knot and then use thread to tie one end of the braid to the other (Fig. 1).

Courting Favor

This project, which I designed along traditional lines, is centered around a God's Eye that is woven around a bare wire core. (As long as you maintain adequate tension on the straws as you weave, the wire won't show through.) The God's-Eye weave that you're about to learn is also used in other projects in this book.

Challenge Rating

Time Rating

MATERIALS

2 pieces of medium-gauge wire, each 6" (15.2cm) long
   God's Eye

48 long straws without heads
   God's Eye

8 long straws with large heads
   Heart

36 long straws without heads
   Heart border

8 long straws with heads
   Love Knots (two)

TECHNIQUES

Scaffold knot (page 21)

God's Eye (see this section)

Four-Straw FTG (pages 30-31)

Batwing (page 47)

Adding new straws to Batwings (see this section)

Two Straws at Four Corners (page 36)

Love Knots (page 73)

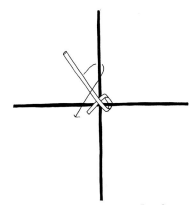

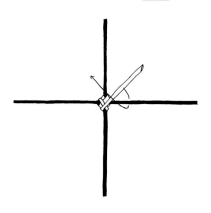

FIG. 2

Using a scaffold knot (Fig. 5 on page 21), tie the two wires at right angles to each other.

With your thumb and index finger, hold the wire cross in the center. (You'll need to maintain this grip until you've completed the first four folds.) Place the first straw over the center of the cross, with one short section extending between the bottom and left-hand wires and the longer section extending between the top and right-hand wires.

Holding the straw in place over the wires and using Figure 2 as a guide, first wrap the longer straw section under the right-hand wire and up to extend between the top and left-hand wires, keeping the wrap as close as possible to the wire center. Then wrap the straw under the top wire (the next wire counterclockwise) and up to extend between the bottom and left-hand wires. Repeat, moving one wire counterclockwise and wrapping the straw under the wire and up each time.

As you continue to weave counterclockwise around the wires, you'll need to insert new straws. When the old straw becomes too short or too thick, trim it off at an angle, about 1/8" (3 mm) beyond the wire arm (Fig. 3), and position a new straw inside it. Wrap the new straw under and up, covering the small, protruding section of the old straw to help create a good, tight hold. Remember not to wait too long to insert a new straw, or the varying diameters of the old and new straws will make the weave look uneven.

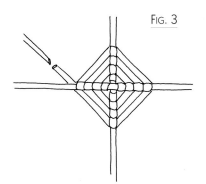

FIG. 3

Continue until your God's Eye is 4" x 4" (10.2 x 10.2 cm). Wrap the last straw behind the weave and tie it to the wrapped wire with thread. Set this completed portion of the project aside, covering it with a damp towel.

Next, to make the heart shape, weave two 7"-long (17.8 cm) Four-Straw FTG plaits. Stretch each plait to 9" (22.9 cm) to give it a chainlike quality. Instead of tying off the ends of these braids, use clothespins to keep the straws from unraveling.

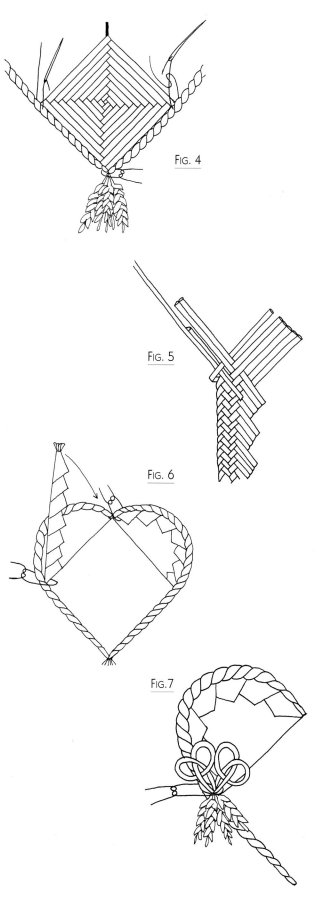

FIG. 4

FIG. 5

FIG. 6

FIG. 7

Uncover the God's Eye and position it so that it forms a diamond shape. Bend its left and right sides upward to make the diamond concave. Tie the starting points of the FTG plaits to the bottom corner of the God's Eye, with the wheat heads hanging down. Run the plaits up along the bottom edges of the diamond. To attach the plaits to the two outside corners, use a wide-eyed needle to run a length of thread through the middle of each plait. Then knot the threads behind the wires so they won't be visible at the front of the project (Fig. 4). Remove the clothespins from the FTG plaits, shape their upper sections to form the heart, and tie their ends to the top of the diamond.

The inner edge of the upper portion of the heart is bordered with two 6"-long (15.2 cm) Batwing plaits. As you weave these, you'll probably need to insert new straws. This is always done on the left. As you can see in Figure 5, the outermost left-hand straw is folded over the second outermost left-hand straw and under the rest in that group. Insert the new straw when this second outermost straw from the left begins to get short. Place a new straw on top of it, overlapping the two by about 1" (2.5 cm). Fold the outermost left-hand straw as usual, covering both the old and new straws before moving it under the rest.

When you've finished these plaits, tie them to the right and left corners of the diamond, shape them to meet the inner edges of the FTG plaits, and then tie their other ends to the top of the diamond (Fig. 6). Trim any straw ends that protrude from the Batwing plaits. Now bend the four excess wire lengths extending from the corners of the diamond to lie flat and behind it.

Next, weave four 6" (15.2 cm) lengths of Two Straws at Four Corners plait. Shape each one into a Love Knot and tie the Knots together in pairs. Tie one pair to each outer corner of the diamond shape, adjusting it so that the inner loops form a heart shape (Fig. 7). If you'd like to add more wheat heads to the base of the project, just add a column of straws to its back surface, tying them at the base and top of the diamond.

The Sentinel

MORGYN GEOFFRY OWENS-CELLI
Made specifically for a retrospective of the
author's work at the Smithsonian's Renwick Gallery,
the Sentinel is now part of the collection of the
American Museum of Straw Art.
Photo courtesy of photographer Michael G. Patton

Sweetheart

This simple project, thought to be Welsh in origin, was given as a token of the heart to ensure good fortune in all matters of love. The Sweetheart is made from a single bunch of straws. One section of the bunch forms the central column, and two other sections are used to weave the Hair Braids that make up the heart.

MATERIALS

15 to 20 large-diameter straws with large heads
Heart and column

3 straws with heads
Hanger

TECHNIQUES

Three-Straw Hair Braid (pages 28-29)

Tie together 15 to 20 straws (depending on their size and variety). Separate out from this bunch three straws on the left and three on the right; you'll make a Hair Braid with each set of three. To form the column, tie together the remaining straws, 3" (7.6 cm) from the first tie. Trim off these column straws about 1-1/2" (3.9 cm) from the last tie.

With each set of three straws, weave a 7"-long (17.8 cm) Hair Braid, but rather than tying the braids off when you're finished, use clothespins to keep their ends from unraveling. Shape the two Hair Braids into a heart, remove the clothes-pins, and tie them to the column, over the tie at the 3" mark (Fig. 8).

Bend the excess straw lengths at the end of each Hair Braid down the front of the column and tie them to it just above the wheat heads. Trim the straw ends close to the knot.

To make the looped hanger, weave a 5"-long (12.7 cm) Three-Straw Hair Braid, shape it into a loop, and tie it to the top of the heart (Fig. 9). Trim the threads ends and fan out all the wheat heads and the trimmed straw lengths at the top of the column.

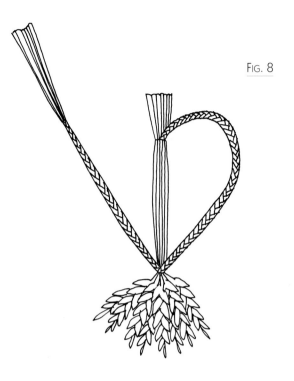

Fig. 8

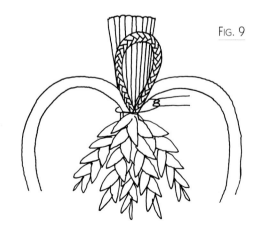

Fig. 9

Devonshire Heart

Originally from Devonshire, England, this heart is a beautiful example of a simple shape that is nevertheless rich and elegant in appearance. Called by some "the heart of eternity," it was given to couples as an anniversary gift, usually after the couple had been married for many years.

Challenge Rating

Time Rating

MATERIALS

20 long, large-diameter straws with heads
  Heart cores (two)

40 long straws with heads
  Heart halves (two)

20 long, large-diameter straws with heads
  Column

8 long, large-diameter straws with heads
  Favors

TECHNIQUES

Five-Straw Spiral (pages 48-49)

Adding new straws to Spirals (page 51)

Compass Weave (pages 32-33)

FIG. 10

The Devonshire Heart is made with two sections of Five-Straw Spiral plait, each woven around a ten-straw core. The plaits are shaped and tied to make a heart and are then attached to a twenty-straw column.

To start each Spiral, make a core by tying ten thick straws together at the base and again 7" (17.8 cm) above that point. Don't trim the straws just yet. Tie five straws to the core and weave a Five-Straw Spiral up around its full 7" length, making sure to add new straws so that the finished Spiral will have long lengths of straw remaining at one end. Tie off each Spiral at the 7" point, but don't trim the ends of the core straws or leftover working straws yet.

To shape the heart, first tie the ends (not the starting points) of the two Spirals together. Then bring the starting point of each Spiral down one side of the untrimmed core straws, shaping the Spiral to form one half of the heart. Tie the starting point of each Spiral to the untrimmed core straws, 3" (7.6 cm) down from the crown of the heart (Fig. 10). Because the Spirals are fairly thick, you'll have to bend them as you tie them into place. You may also need to adjust the heart shape after it has been completely tied. Trim away the core straws close to the knot and set the heart aside.

To make the twenty-straw column, tie together 20 straws with large heads. Tie them again, 3" above the first tie. Turn the heart face down on your work surface. Position the twenty-straw column over the heart, aligning it with the heart's core straws and placing the heads of the column straws over the heads of the heart. Tie the column to the crown and base of the heart. (Note that the trimmed ends of the heart's core straws will now be hidden between these two layers of wheat heads.)

FIG. 11

Two favors are attached to the back of this project. Although they're barely visible from the front, they help to spread out the spray of heads. To make these favors, use eight very long, large-diameter straws with heads to make two Compass Weave plaits. Tie each plait into a loop and tie the two loops together so that the heads of each one are centered in the middle of the other. Referring to Figure 11, attach the favors to the back of the assembled heart, at its base. (To keep the favors perpendicular to the core, run the threads around the front of the heart and through the points of the loops.)

If you wish to create a hanger for the Devonshire Heart, weave a 3"-long plait, using only a few straws, and attach it to the back of the heart, at the crown.

Double Mordiford Heart

Each separate heart design in the Double Mordiford represents one of the two individuals in love. The combined designs make up a new one, which represents the couple's loving union. Double Mordiford Hearts can be made with Four-, Six-, or Seven-Straw FTG plaits. A stretched four-straw version is presented here.

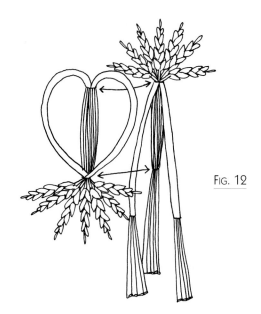

FIG. 12

MATERIALS

16 long, large-diameter straws with large heads
   Hearts (two)

20 long, large-diameter straws with large heads
   Cores (two)

TECHNIQUES

Four-Straw FTG (pages 30-31)

This project is made with four FTG plaits. Two are attached to one core to form a heart. The other two are attached to a separate core, and after the cores are joined, the second pair of plaits is looped through the first pair to make interlocking hearts.

Using straws with heads, start by making four, stretched Four-Straw FTG plaits, each about 7" (17.8 cm) long. Leave the working straws untrimmed. Next, make a core by tying ten straws together below the heads and again about 3" (7.6 cm) from that point. Tie the starting points of two of the braids to the end of the core where the heads are located.

Shape these two braids into a heart and tie their ends over the 3" tie on the core. Bend down the untrimmed straws at the end of each braid so that they're parallel and next to the core. Then tie them to the core.

Make another ten-straw core with heads. Attach the starting points of the second pair of braids to this second core. Leave the other ends of these two plaits temporarily unattached.

Place the first heart (back side down) on top of the incomplete heart, as shown in Figure 12. Tie the two cores together at the points indicated by the arrows in this illustration.

Now pull the loose arms of the incomplete heart up through the loops of the first heart (Fig. 13) and tie them to the bottom of the first heart. Bend the excess straws at the ends of these braids parallel to the core and tie them in place at the crown of the first heart. Trim any excess lengths of straw near the crowns so that you can see the hearts clearly. Also trim any other straws as necessary and fan out the heads at each end to dry.

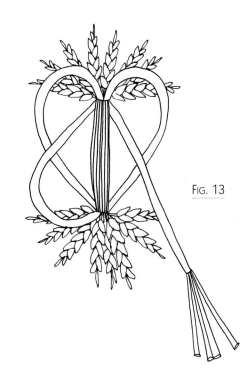

FIG. 13

Ancient and Traditional Projects

So-called "ancient" designs can be divided into two main categories: designs that originated centuries ago and have been passed down through the generations virtually unchanged; and those that suggest a primitive or ancient character even though they're actually contemporary in design. We tend to think of traditional designs as ones that haven't changed much over time, but this design category includes many that are only four or five generations old, as well as designs that each generation has changed just slightly.

Earth Mother

*Many ancient wheat-woven designs were born from a belief
in an Earth Mother. In this design, I've combined primitive
elements of African and Indo-European Earth Mother figures.*

MATERIALS

22 long, large-diameter straws with large heads
Headdress/part of skirt

25 long, large-diameter straws without heads
Head and body

6 long straws with heads
Core for arms

16 long straws without heads
Arms

14 large-diameter straws without heads
Bodice

50 long, large-diameter straws without heads
Skirt

3 long, small-diameter straws with small heads
Belt

TECHNIQUES

Corizon (pages 64-65)

Ribbon-plait locking (page 39)

Four-Straw Spiral (page 50)

Adding new straws to Spirals (page 51)

Seven-Straw Ribbon (page 39)

Three-Straw Hair Braid (pages 28-29)

Start the Earth Mother by weaving a 22-straw Corizon to serve as her headdress. After you've added the last two straws and brought each one down to lock it, you'll note that the straw on the left is unsecured by any other straws. Holding the Corizon carefully so the straws don't shift positions, examine the two surfaces, select the one you think looks best, and turn that surface up. (No matter which side of the Corizon you choose as the front, there will always be an unsecured straw in the left-hand group.)

All the straw ends without heads must now be locked in the same manner as Ribbon plaits are locked. Begin by lifting the second straw from the outside of the left-hand group and passing the outermost, unsecured left-hand straw under it and over all of the rest in that group. Replace the lifted straw. Repeat this locking motion until all the straws on the left have been passed over to the right. (The outermost straw of this group will lack a straw under which to pass; just fold it over to rest with the previously locked straws.)

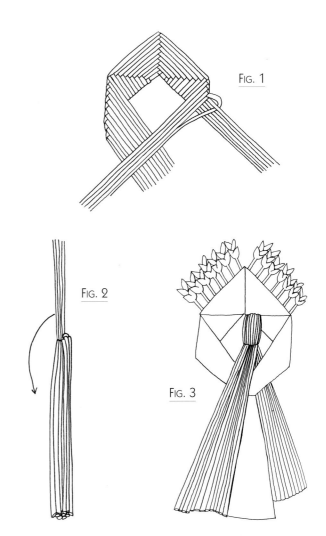

FIG. 1

FIG. 2

FIG. 3

Now, using the same manipulation and Figure 1 as a guide, lock the straws in the right-hand group toward the left. These straws will pass over the ends of the straws that have just been locked from the left, and the straws in the two groups will intersect just under the center of the Corizon. Tie the straws together at this point, holding them flat and side by side as you tighten the knot so they don't bunch up. The excess straw lengths below this tie will form part of the Earth Mother's skirt.

To make the body and head of the Earth Mother, tie 25 straws together at the half-way point. Holding the tied straws vertically in one hand, begin folding down the straws in the upper half to cover those in the lower half (Fig. 2). To ensure even distribution of the straws, turn the column as you fold. When you're finished, tie the column about 1" (2.5 cm) from its top to form the Earth Mother's head.

Spread the straws extending from below the tied "neck" in half and insert one half through the hole of the Corizon so that the Corizon extends above the head (Fig. 3). Push the body all the way down so that the head rests well within the

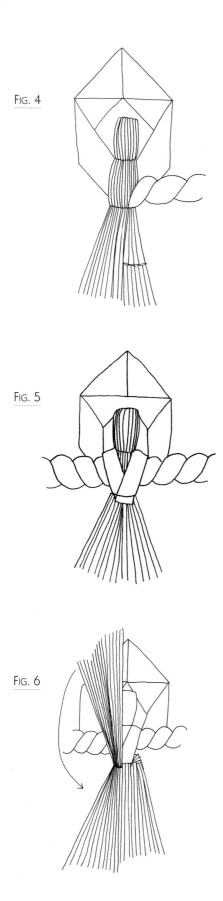

FIG. 4

FIG. 5

FIG. 6

Corizon opening. Tie the divided straws to the Corizon, over the tie that binds the intersecting Corizon straws. Set this portion of your work aside.

Each arm is made with a Four-Straw Spiral plait that is woven around a three-straw core. Start by tying together three straws near the heads and again 3" (7.6 cm) from that point. Then tie four straws at three corners of the core. Weave the Spiral, covering the full 3" of the core and inserting straws as necessary. (You'll need plenty of unwoven straw length at the end of the Spiral.) Tie the arm off with thread, but do not trim the excess thread lengths. Repeat to make another arm.

Bend the unwoven straws of each arm down at a right angle, and attach these bent straws to the body by tying them at the tie that binds the body to the Corizon (Fig. 4). You may need to use a needle to run your thread through the top of the body so that the knot doesn't pull the Corizon head-dress into the body.

To make the bodice, first weave two Seven-Straw Ribbon plaits, each 4" to 5" (10.2 to 12.7 cm) long. Tie one end of each to the back of the body and wrap the plaits diagonally over the shoulders and diagonally down the front of the fig-ure (Fig. 5). These plaits, which cross each other in the front and back, will help hold the arms in place. Tie both plaits to the body.

The skirt, which gives the Earth Mother her bountiful look, is made with 50 straws. Tie these around the waist of the figure, over the ties of the bodice plaits, so that equal por-tions of the straws extend above and below the waist. Now fold the upper portions of the skirt straws down, bending the straws about 1/4" (6 mm) above the waist tie (Fig. 6). Space them evenly around the figure and don't allow any to cross over others or bunch up. (You may find it easier work with two batches of 25 straws each, as these smaller num-bers will be easier to attach securely and fold evenly.)

Secure the folded straws temporarily with masking tape or a rubber band. Then, using doubled, very strong linen thread, tie the straws 1/4" (6 mm) below the tie that secured the skirt straws to the body. This tie will make the straws flare out to form a narrow platform at the top of the skirt. Remove the tape or rubber band and flare the lower skirt straws to enlarge the skirt.

The last tie you made will be disguised by a belt (or girdle). Weave a Three-Straw Hair Braid at least 10" to 12" (25.4 to 30.5 cm) long. Wrap the finished braid around the waist once or twice and tie it under one arm, with the heads drap-ing down as shown in the photo. Finish off by trimming any uneven straws from the hem of the skirt.

Celtic Knot

Cora Hendershot

Glory Braid

The broom-shaped Glory Braid, a variation of the Hair Braid, is an old weave, one that was hung in homes to sweep away evil and bring in friends. Although no one is sure how this braid acquired its name, people in Devonshire, England believe that it was derived from an old and popular English saying: "To have a house filled with friends is a glory indeed!" Whatever its origin, this simple little piece will be a glory in your repertoire of wheat weavings.

Although it's a simple weave, the Glory is often executed clumsily. When woven correctly, the folds must create a flat edge on each side of the plait. Use a thick-walled wheat variety, one which will offer a healthy resistance to bending and yield the required crisp, flat edges.

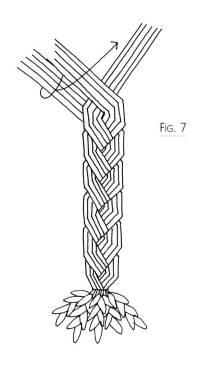

FIG. 7

Challenge Rating

Time Rating

MATERIALS

12 long, large-diameter straws with large heads
   Entire piece

(Black bearded wheat recommended for its thick walls)

TECHNIQUES

Hair Braids (pages 28-30)

The main difference between this weave and the usual Hair Braid is the number of straws in each group (Fig. 7). How you move the groups of straws will determine your success.

Tie twelve straws together and divide them into three groups of four. As you move these groups in typical Hair-Braid fashion, keep the four straws in each group in the same order. To ensure that the straws in the group you're bending remain flat and side by side, use the group in the middle as a guide by holding the straws in it stationary each time you bend a group over it.

To maintain control over the bending process, hold the straws about 1" (2.5 cm) above the area of the bend. Rather than lifting up the straws sharply as you bend them, slide them horizontally over the middle group, keeping them in the same plane and pushing them slightly back toward your body as you move them. Doing so will help crease the straws at the proper angle and ensure a crisp edge at the folds.

Complete nine folds on each side. To finish off, first fold the middle group and then each of the other groups under the braid so that the straw ends rest behind the starting tie near the heads. Tie the straws off at this point. Make a looped ribbon hanger and tie a bow near the base.

Sunspray

Farmers valued the sun for its role in ripening crops, so it's no surprise that solar symbols
appear in some traditional designs. These sun symbols naturally became associated with
wealth. They were hung near the doors of homes in order to promote good business and
near the doors of barns to promote farming prosperity. In many cultures, the weavings
also represented manhood. The design presented here includes variations of my own.

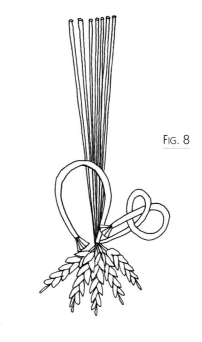

FIG. 8

MATERIALS

14 long straws with heads
   Entire piece

TECHNIQUES

Three-Straw Hair Braid (pages 28-29)

Four-Straw FTG (pages 30-31)

Love Knots (page 73)

Welsh Harp (pages 60-61)

Tie together 14 straws and divide them in half. Using the innermost straws in the left-hand group, weave 6" to 7" (15.2 to 17.8 cm) of Three-Straw Hair Braid. Rather than tying the braid off, temporarily secure the end with a clothespin.

With the remaining four straws in the left-hand group, make an equal length of Four-Straw FTG plait. This design is most often created with a stretched version of this plait. Whether or not you choose to stretch the braid, make sure that its finished length is 6" to 7".

Bring the end of the FTG plait to the starting point of the tied straws, shaping the plait to form either the traditional round loop or—as today's wheat weavers often prefer—an oval (Fig. 8). Tie the end of the braid in place.

While holding the end of the Hair Braid, remove the clothespin and tie the braid into a Love Knot. Secure the end of this braid to the starting point as well.

Trim the straws of the braids to any desired length. (In some solar designs, a few of the straw ends are left longer to represent more rays of the Sun.)

To create the pattern of bent straws at the top of the Sunspray, start by tying together the seven straws of the right-hand group at a point 2-1/2" (6.4 cm) from the base. Turn the project over and position a straightedge or ruler across the straws, 1-1/2" (3.8 cm) from this second tie. Bend the straws up and over its sharp edge to crease them.

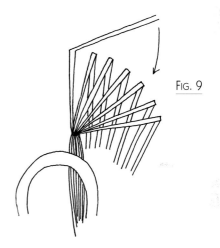

FIG. 9

Make sure that the ruler rests flat on the work surface and that the straws are flat and side by side as you do this. Pinch each straw at the crease.

Referring to Figure 9, which shows the following process from the front of the project rather than from the back, bring the first bent straw down to the base to form an angle of slightly less than 90 degrees. Bring the next bent straw down to the right of the previous straw to form a smaller angle. Continue bending all the creased straws down, positioning each one to form smaller and smaller angles. Tie the bent straws to the starting point and trim their ends evenly.

Devonshire Neck

The Devonshire Neck, which is described in some detail on page 12, is one of the oldest designs in wheat weaving. It is sometimes called the Master Weave, possibly because it isn't as easy to make as many other designs, but more likely because the "master weaver" of a town may have been the only person permitted to make it. Certainly, by the time the harvest lads incorporated the Neck into their harvest customs, it had lost this honor.

Challenge Rating   Time Rating

MATERIALS

25 long, large-diameter straws with heads
    Three-layer core

50 long straws without heads
    Three-layer core

60 to 75 long straws (5 with heads)
    Spiral

TECHNIQUES

Five-Straw Spiral (pages 48-49)

Adding new straws to Spirals (page 51)

The core around which the Spiral is woven is constructed in three layers so that it varies in width along its length. To make it, you must have a specific number of straws on hand, so be sure to count them carefully.

Start by tying together at the base 25 very thick, long straws with heads. Tie the straws together again 10" (25.4 cm) from the first tie. Trim the ends of the straws, beyond the knot, leaving four straws untrimmed in the center of the bundle. (These longer straws will help give some substance to the finished handle.)

To make the next layer of the core, space 25 straws without heads evenly around the existing core and tie them at 2-1/2" (6.4 cm) and 7-1/2" (19.1 cm) from the bottom of the existing core (Fig. 10). Don't make these knots too tight; the ties should indent the straws slightly but shouldn't force them to jut out at angles. Using scissors, carefully trim the straws close to the ties to make even edges at the ends of this layer. Avoid cutting into the first core section.

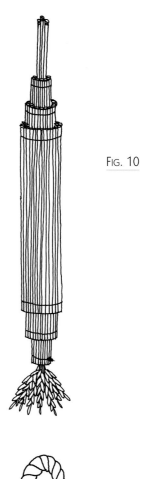

FIG. 10

To create the last layer of the core, space another 25 straws without heads around the second layer and tie them off at 3-3/4" (9.5 cm) and 6-1/4" (15.9 cm) from the bottom end of the first layer. Trim the top and bottom of this last layer of straws as before.

The width of the core will control the width of the Five-Straw Spiral that you weave around it. Begin by tying five straws with heads to the base of the narrowest section of core. Then weave the Spiral up around the entire core, remembering to move the straws at the proper angles, adding straws as necessary, and continuing right over the end of the smallest-diameter core. Continue to weave 5" (12.7 cm) of additional Spiral around the four untrimmed straws extending from the center of the narrowest core, and then, using a long piece of thread, tie off the working straws and the four untrimmed straws, and trim the thread ends. Cut the ends of the straws about 1/2" (1.3 cm) from this tie.

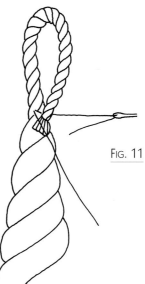

FIG. 11

To form the looped hanger, bring the end of the narrow Spiral down to the point at which the Spiral started to extend over the top of the core. Stitch the hanger between the rounds of the spiral so that the thread passes around the inside core to secure the loop (Fig. 11). Trim the threads ends close to the knot.

John Barleycorn Favor

The name of this traditional favor is a term once commonly used to personify the grain from which malt liquor was made. The design, originally created to celebrate the joy of life, has lost favor over the last several generations, but it certainly had its day. A wide variety of plaits have been used to make it, indicating that the design was a popular one. Its shape—two linked loops extending from opposite sides of a woven central column—has never varied.

In the project presented here, the column consists of a Thirteen-Straw Stacked Spiral Link, and the loops are made with Rustic and Four-Straw FTG plaits.

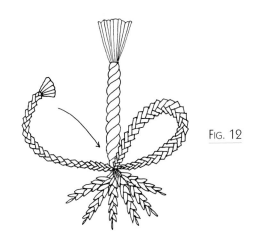

FIG. 12

Challenge Rating Time Rating

MATERIALS

13 small-diameter straws with heads
  Column and core

1 piece of medium-gauge wire, 4" (7.6 cm) long
  Column and core

8 long straws with heads
  Bottom loops

8 small-diameter straws with heads
  Top loops

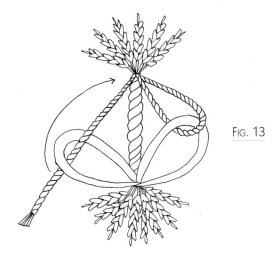

FIG. 13

TECHNIQUES

Thirteen-Straw Stacked Spiral Link (page 52)

or Five-Straw Spiral (pages 48-49)

Rustic (page 43)

Four-Straw FTG (pages 30-31)

To start making the column, tie thirteen straws with heads around a bare wire core and weave a 3"-long (7.6 cm) Thirteen-Straw Stacked Spiral Link plait or any round plait with at least seven straws in it. (A Five-Straw Spiral plait will work, but weave it around a core that is thicker than the wire core used in the Thirteen-Straw Stacked Spiral Link.) Tie off the column when you've finished weaving.

To make the first two loops (shown at the bottom of the photo), weave two 6"-long (15.2 cm) four-straw Rustic

plaits. Tie off the ends of each and trim the excess straws. Tie the starting point of each plait to opposite sides of the starting point of the column. Bend the braids up to form loops and attach their ends to the front of the column (Fig. 12). Fan out the heads of the plaits along with the heads of the column.

Now weave two Four-Straw FTG plaits, stretching each one to 6" in length. Don't tie these off; use clothespins to keep them from unraveling. Attach the starting point of each FTG plait to the other end of the column, with the plait heads above the column and the woven section extending downward.

To link the two sets of plaits, bring the ends of the FTG plaits up through the Rustic loops and back to the top of the column before tying them off to form loops (Fig. 13). Trim the straws ends and fan out the wheat heads at this end of the column.

Celtic Harp

The harp has long been a folk symbol for the sharing of news, one which may have originated with the troubadours who wandered about Europe sharing the news of the day. As is the case with many musical instruments, the harp also represents joy.

Straw harps have been created for many generations. In Germany, straw angels often hold the harps, while in Ireland, harps serve as a national emblem. In some areas of Europe, these designs have come to represent wealth. No one is sure why, but harps—especially grand harps—were not inexpensive.

This design—a grand harp—differs from the folk harp of the Irish and other Celtic peoples. It is called a Celtic Harp because its interlacing design elements are typically Celtic in nature.

MATERIALS

20 long straws with heads
Core for Column

25 straws without heads
Spiral column

21 long, large-diameter straws without heads
Harp frame

1 piece of medium-gauge wire, 12" (30.5 cm) long
Harp frame

1 straw without a head
Harp frame

10 long, small-diameter straws with heads
Base platform

12 straws with heads
Loop (bottom)

2 small-diameter straws with heads
Loop (top)

12 large-diameter straws without heads
Harp strings

12 pieces of fine-gauge wire
Harp strings

TECHNIQUES

Five-Straw Spiral (pages 48-49)

Adding new straws to Spirals (page 51)

Seven-Straw Ribbon (page 39)

Adding new straws to Ribbon plaits (see this section)

Ten-Straw Diamond (page 40)

Four-Straw FTG (pages 30-31)

or Two Straws at Four Corners (page 36)

Three-Straw Hair Braid (pages 28-29)

Two Straws at Four Corners (page 36)

Love Knots (page 73)

The column of this project consists of a Five-Straw Spiral plait woven around a straw core. To make the core, tie 20 straws together beneath the heads and again 5" (12.7 cm)

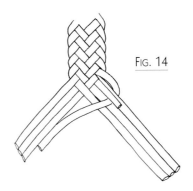

FIG. 14

from that point. You won't be weaving these core straws, so you may want to use a variety with decorative heads.

Using 25 straws without heads, weave the Spiral plait along the full 5" of the column and tie it off at the end of the core. Set the Spiral aside for now.

To make the frame for the harp strings, weave a 12"-long (30.5 cm) Seven-Straw Ribbon plait, adding two full sets of seven new straws each in order to make the desired length. Prepare the two sets of new straws before you start weaving by removing their heads. Be sure to select straws the same diameter as the straws you'll be replacing.

New straws are always inserted to take the place of the second from the outside straw in the right-hand group. Place about 1" (2.5 cm) of the upper end of the new straw under the old straw. Then lift up both the new straw and the old straw above it and pass the outermost right-hand straw under them both and over to the inside of the opposite group (Fig. 14). Lower the new and old straws back onto the work surface and trim the old one to about 1" in length. (When the completed braid has dried, you'll trim off the protruding ends of the old and new straws.)

Lock on the opposite side as usual. Return and lock the added straw by lifting the second straw from the outside and passing the new straw, which is now in the outermost position, across and over to the inside of the opposite group. Leave the short stub of the old straw behind. Doing this will hold the new straw securely in place. In order not to weaken the braid, plan ahead and keep your inserts at some distance from one another. Tie the finished plait off and trim the excess straws at the ends.

The base platform of the harp (visible at the lower left of the photo) is a Ten-Straw Diamond plait made with very delicate

FIG. 15

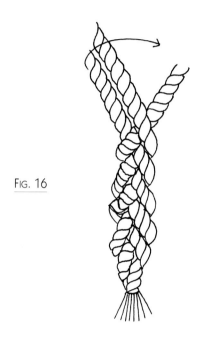

FIG. 16

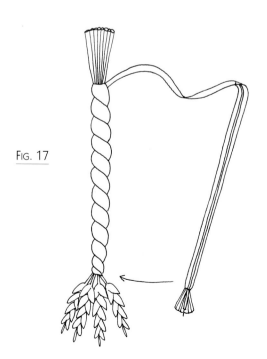

FIG. 17

straws. Tie the ten straws together side by side and weave 5" (12.7 cm) of this plait. Then shape the plait into a loop, with the plait positioned on edge, and tie the two ends together (Fig. 15).

The decorative loop at the lower right of the design is made by interlacing three Four-Straw FTG plaits, each stretched to 5-1/2" (14.0 cm) in length. Weave and stretch the three plaits, tie them together and, using the Hair-Braid technique, braid the sections together very loosely (Fig. 16). (For a beautiful and even more delicate loop, use smaller Two Straws at Four Corners plaits instead.) Tie off the braided plaits at the end and bend the finished braid to form a circle. Set this aside for the moment.

Embellishing the top of the harp is optional. To make the small plaited knot shown at the top of the harp in the photo, weave 4" (10.2 cm) of Two Straws at Four Corners plait and shape it into an open knot as you would with a Love Knot.

To begin construction of the harp, place the platform base to the left of the column and attach it by running a length of thread through the Diamond-plait loop and tying it to the base of the column. (You'll adjust the platform at a right angle when you pin your project to dry.)

To attach the interlaced loop, tie its ends at the base of the column, placing one end at the front of the column and the other at its right side. The interlacing should extend down over the wheat heads.

Before attaching the frame for the harp strings, insert a 12"-long (30.5 cm) piece of wire into a straw and stitch the straw to the flat back surface of the ribbon plait. Then attach the ends of the plait to the top and bottom of the column, checking to see that the wire is located on the inner surface of the plait (Fig. 17).

Add the decorative loop to the top of the column, tying it over the joined plaits to hide their attachment spots. To help maintain the harp's shape as it dries, pin it to a sheet of cardboard or polystyrene foam.

When the harp is completely dry, insert lengths of fine-gauge wire into 11 or 12 straws and cut the straw-covered wires to serve as harp strings. Glue both ends of each of these straws to the inner surface of the Ribbon plait, just behind the wire so the glue won't show from the front.

Folk Angel

The Folk Angel is a beautiful and traditional design, one that symbolizes—as straw angels have for generations—hope and faith in the future. These angels come in a variety of traditional sizes, from small and intricate to large and bold.

Instructions on following pages

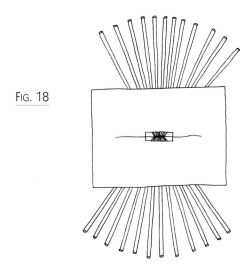

FIG. 18

MATERIALS

12 long, large-diameter straws without heads
  Wings

5 long, large-diameter straws without heads
  Halo

7 long, large-diameter straws without heads
  Arms

26 long, large-diameter straws with small heads
  Body

TECHNIQUES

Chinese Chain Rick Rack (pages 44-45)

Seven-Straw FTG (page 32)

To make the wings, cut the middle 12" (30.5 cm) from each of 12 thick, long straws. Bundle the straws together, evening out the width of this core by turning half of them in one direction and half in the other. Tie the bundle together at its center with a clove-hitch knot, but don't tie the knot tight just yet. First, arrange the straws parallel and side by side on the work surface. Then, using either a ruler, a straightedge, or the cardboard device shown in Figure 18 to hold the straws flat, tighten the thread slowly to form the two wing shapes. Make sure the straws don't bunch up as they're secured.

The halo consists of a modified Chinese Chain Rickrack plait, one which curves inward as it's woven. To make it, you'll change the usual manipulation of the left chain. First, take a good look at Figure 19. In it are shown both the regular manipulation (left) and the modified manipulation (right). In the modification, when you bring the discarded straw #1 up behind straw #4, pull it upward sharply to take up the slack that usually appears in the chain. Then lock it to the right as usual. Notice how doing this takes up the slack in the left chain, visible at the lower left of each illustration. Treating the right chain as usual will make the right side longer than the left and will cause the plait to bend inward as it's worked. Weave the plait until you have

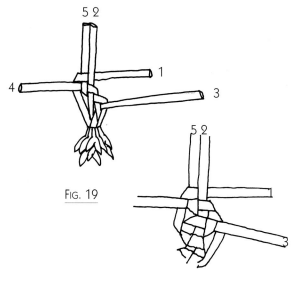

FIG. 19

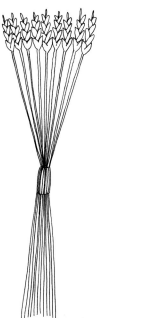

FIG. 20

4

a full circle and the halo is as large as you desire. Tie its ends together.

To make the arms, tie together seven straws without heads and weave them into a 4"-long (10.2 cm) Seven-Straw FTG plait. Tie the plait into a loop and trim the ends to form 1/4"-long (6 mm) hands. Set the loop aside.

Start making the body by bunching together 26 straws with matched heads, aligning their necks carefully. Tie the straws tightly together, 5" (12.7 cm) below the necks. Tie them once more, about 1" (2.5 cm) below the first tie, but only tightly enough to indent the straws slightly (Fig. 20). Trim the thread ends from the two knots.

Position this bunch of wheat with the heads facing away from you. The 1"-long portion between the two ties will become the back of the angel's head. Referring to Figure 21, lift up four evenly-spaced straws from the back of the bundle, insert the halo, and bring the four straws down, making sure they hide the halo's tied ends.

Now lift up another six straws underneath this area and slide the angel wings underneath them. Without changing the positions of the straws in the wings, push the wings up as far as possible toward the head. Hold the wings securely in place and turn the angel over. Lift up six straws at the front of the body and slip them through the arm loop, pushing the loop up under the head (Fig. 22).

To secure all the parts, tie a tight knot just under the wings and arms; this tie will form the angel's waist. Before folding down the straws above the angel to form her hair and dress (Fig. 23), pull down one straw only in order to see how much you'll need to trim from the body straws underneath in order to make them 1/2" (1.3 cm) shorter than the length of the straw you just folded down. Trim the body straws next. Then tie together the loose ends of the body straws about 1" (2.5 cm) above their ends.

Now fold down the remaining heads and straws, locating half of them on each side of the angel. Tie these straws tightly at the waist. Doing so will make the wheat heads fan out to form the bottom of the skirt.

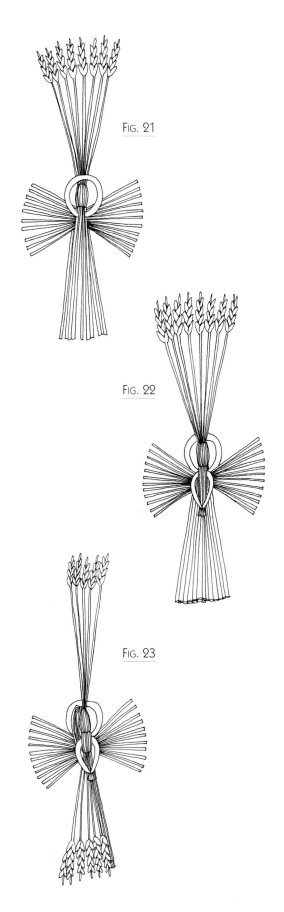

FIG. 21

FIG. 22

FIG. 23

Chapter

7

Projects
from the
Harvest Time

In one sense, it's possible to view all wheat weaving as having been born from the harvest, as the art form itself has ancient, worldwide cultural ties to the reaping of grain. Some designs, however, are more specifically related than others to harvest customs and beliefs. You'll find a sampling of them in this chapter.

Harvest

Some of the most beautiful wheat weavings are among the simplest in design. Many of these are probably very old in origin and were first made at a time when their symbolic function was their most important aspect. The Harvest is such a design.

For those fascinated by ancient folk customs, the Harvest is a rich source of pleasure indeed. Its oval shape is an ancient symbol representing women, and the entire design suggests a primitive figurine—one with arms outstretched at its sides. The simple Spiral plait adds to the overall beauty of the design.

Challenge Rating

Time Rating

MATERIALS

28 long straws with heads
    Cores for oval (two)

2 pieces of medium-gauge wire, each 5" (12.7 cm) long
    Cores for oval (two)

30 long straws with heads
    Plaits for oval (two)

26 long straws with heads
    Column

TECHNIQUES

Five-Straw Spiral (pages 48-49)

Adding new straws to Spirals (page 51)

The oval shape consists of two Five-Straw Spiral plaits, each woven around a straw-and-wire core. Start by gathering together 14 medium- to large-diameter straws with heads. Insert a 5" (12.7 cm) length of wire into the bundle of straws, pushing about 1/2" (1.3 cm) of the wire into the straw heads. Tie the straws and wire together just beneath the necks.

Pull five working straws out from among the core straws, spacing them at four corners. Tie the remaining core straws together 4" (10.2 cm) from the first tie. About 1/2" of the bottom end of the wire should extend beyond this knot. Trim the straw ends to 1/2" in length; their ends should align with the end of the wire.

Using the working straws you pulled down, weave the Spiral plait to cover the full length of the 4"-long core, inserting new straws as necessary for a clean smooth look. Tie off the end of the Spiral and set it aside. Repeat to make another Spiral the same length.

Tie the two Spirals together as shown in Figure 1, with the trimmed straw ends of each one hidden behind the heads of the other. Bend the tied pieces to open them up into an oval shape measuring 2" to 3" (5.1 to 7.6 cm) from top to bottom (not from end to end). The wire inside the core will help maintain the shape.

To make the column, tie 26 straws together near the heads. Tie them again at exactly the same distance from the first tie as the top and bottom of the oval are far apart—2" to 3".

Turn the oval over so that the trimmed straws at each end are facing up. Place the column on top of the oval and insert two straight pins between the rounds of each Spiral to mark the center top and bottom spots. Remove the column and thread a sewing needle with heavy carpet or linen thread. Insert the needle between the Spiral rounds at one pin-marked location, running it around the interior core of the Spiral and out between rounds. (The thread shouldn't show at the front of the project.) Repeat at the other pin-marked location and remove the straight pins.

Replace the column and knot the thread ends to secure the oval by pulling it firmly in place (Fig. 2). Trim the column straws approximately 8" (20.3 cm) below the bottom of the oval and flare out the ends of the straws.

Osburn Crown

Crowns are traditional harvest designs, which most folk historians agree were probably born as decorations that appeared at harvest celebrations. The woven designs may originally have been straw replicas of the crowns worn by harvest queens or may simply have been made as the "crowning" achievements of the harvest. Some crowns were made to honor people connected with the harvest. Contemporary weaver Kathie Osburn has created this crown in keeping with age-old traditions.

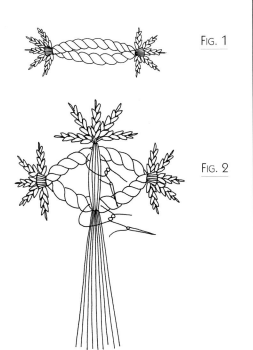

FIG. 1

FIG. 2

Instructions on following page

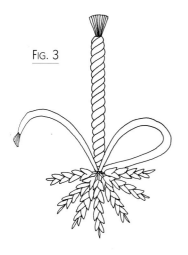

FIG. 3

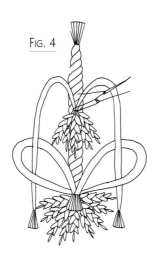

FIG. 4

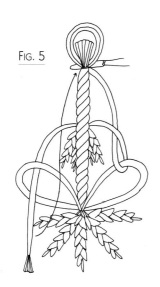

FIG. 5

MATERIALS

9 long straws with heads
Column

14 long straws with heads
Crown loops (two; bottom)

8 long straws with heads
Crown loops (two; center)

4 straws without heads
Uppermost loops (two)

14 straws without heads
Two straw bows

TECHNIQUES

Nine-Straw Grouped Link (pages 51-52)

Seven-Straw FTG (page 32)

Four-Straw FTG (pages 30-31)

Two Straws at Three Corners (page 36)

Straw bows (page 138)

Before assembling this project, you'll weave its various parts. To make the vertical column in its center, weave a 5" (12.7 cm) length of Nine-Straw Grouped Link plait, tying and trimming the straw ends about 1" (2.5 cm) beyond the knot. Set this piece aside.

Next, make the two loops at the bottom of the crown by weaving two Seven-Straw FTG plaits, each 6" to 6-1/2" (15.2 to 16.5 cm) long. (You may want to create slightly shorter plaits and stretch them to the required length.)

To make the two loops at the center of the crown, weave two Four-Straw FTG plaits, each 6" to 6-1/2" in length. (Don't stretch these braids.)

The doubled loop at the top of the Osburn Crown consists of a pair of Two Straws at Three Corners plaits. First make one 4" (10.2 cm) long. Trim its ends close to the knots, form the plait into a loop, and tie its ends together. Repeat to make another plait that is long enough to surround the loop you just made. Shape the second plait around the first loop and tie the two loops together at their tips.

Assembly of this project is relatively easy. First, referring to Figure 3, shape the Seven-Straw FTG plaits into loops and tie them to the base of the column, securing their starting points at its front and turning the column over in order to tie the ends of the plaits to its back.

Next, thread a wide-eyed needle. Turn the column face down and arrange the heads of the Four-Straw FTG plaits as shown in Figure 4, 2" to 2-1/2" (5.1 to 6.4 cm) above the column's starting point. Run the needle through and out the column back and knot the thread ends around the starting points of the two plaits.

Turn the column over and, referring to Figure 5, bring the ends of the Four-Straw FTG plaits to the top of the column by pulling them up through the lower loops and then under themselves. Tie the plait ends to the top of the column, one on each side. Also tie the doubled loop to the top rear of the column.

For added texture and decoration, tie one straw bow to the base of the column and one to the top.

Pennsylvania Harvest Hex Sign

The beautiful barns of the Pennsylvania countryside often display traditional hex symbols near their roofs. Painted on the wood or carved into it, these designs were thought to protect the farm and its occupants. Wheat farmers sometimes made similar hex symbols with straw. The design presented here is based on traditional Pennsylvania German folk symbols.

Challenge Rating   Time Rating

MATERIALS

8 long straws without heads
  Rustic loops (two)

14 long straws without heads
  Ribbon loops (two)

16 long, large-diameter straws without heads
  Compass Weave loops (four)

42 straws without heads
  Arms (two)

2 pieces of medium-gauge wire, each 8" (20.3 cm) long
  Arms (two)

1 straw split
  Center

1 small piece of manila folder or buff-colored envelope
  Center

TECHNIQUES

Rustic (page 43)

Seven-Straw Ribbon (page 39)

Compass Weave (pages 32-33)

Straw-covered wires (page 33)

Pull-Over plait (see this section)

Appliqué (pages 21-22)

The Harvest Hex Sign shown here is made up of two arms, eight interlocking oval loops, and a split-covered paper circle. When working with this many elements, it's essential to let the various parts dry before gluing them together.

Start by making two four-straw Rustic plaits, each 5-1/4" (13.3 cm) long. Tie off the ends and shape each plait into an oval, but don't tie the ends together yet. Pin the shaped loops onto cardboard or rigid polystyrene foam and allow to dry.

Next, make two Seven-Straw Ribbon plaits, each 5-1/4" long. Shape and pin to dry as before.

Weave four Compass Weave plaits, each 7-1/4" (18.4 cm) long. Shape and pin to dry.

The four arms of the project consist of two straw-covered wire cores, each of which is woven with a pair of arrow-shaped Pull-Over plaits. You haven't learned to make these plaits yet, so read the instructions that follow before starting.

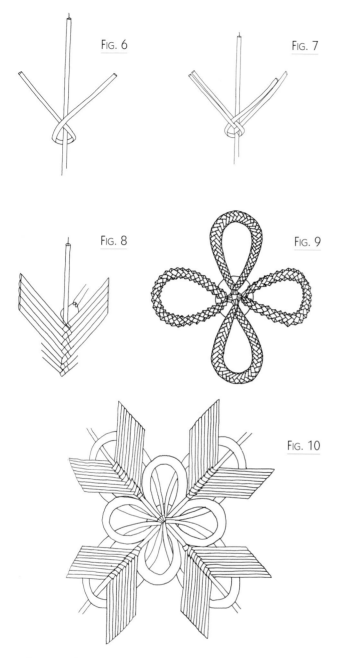

FIG. 6

FIG. 7

FIG. 8

FIG. 9

FIG. 10

Pull the straw to tighten it; the straw ends should form a V shape when you're finished.

Next, take a good look at Figure 7, which shows the placement and manipulation of the next straw. Holding the first straw so that it won't unravel, position the next straw on top of the core, above the left-hand portion of the first straw. (Note that its right-hand portion will cover the right-hand portion of the first straw.) Wrap the right-hand portion of the second straw behind the core, under the left-hand portion of the first straw, and over its own left-hand portion to rest above the right-hand portion of the first straw.

To add the next and subsequent straws to this plait, place each one above the last added. Bring the new straw's right-hand portion over the right-hand straw immediately beneath it, behind the core, up between the two uppermost left-hand straw portions, and back to rest at the top of the right-hand group. Tie off the last straw, doing so from behind to hide the knot (Fig. 8). Trim the ends of the straws evenly.

Now repeat the same process, starting 3" (7.6 cm) from the other end of the arm to make a second Pull-Over plait. Finally, make another complete arm by weaving a Pull-Over plait at each end of another straw-covered wire core.

To make the appliqué circle, first cut a 3/4"-diameter (1.9 cm) circle from a manila folder or buff-colored envelope. Review the section on appliqué and prepare one split before proceeding. Spread craft glue smoothly over one face of the paper circle. Place the split across the glue-covered surface, pressing it into the glue for a firm bond. Turn the circle over and trim off the ends of the split at the circle's edge. Turn the circle onto its back and, using one of the trimmed split ends, add another split to the circle's front face. Trim this split in the same fashion. Continue until the face of the circle is covered with splits.

Wipe away any excess glue. Using a burnishing tool, rub the split-covered surface well. Turn the circle face down again and trim its edges carefully by cutting through the manila paper to make a slightly smaller split-covered circle.

Place the completed circle face down on your work surface and glue the tips of the two Rustic loops and the two Seven-Straw Ribbon plait loops to its center (Fig. 9).

Next, tie the two arms of the Pull-Over plaits together at right angles to make a plus-sign shape. Glue the joined arms to the back of the circle, on top of the loops.

With the circle still facing down, position the Compass Weave plaits as shown in Figure 10, noting that their looped sections cover the arms and their ends run up through the Rustic and Ribbon plait loops. To complete the project, glue the ends of the Compass Weave plaits to the back of the circle.

To begin making the arms, insert an 8" (20.3 cm) length of wire into a straw and trim the straw ends to match the wire length. Next, cut ten pieces of straw, each 4" (10.2 cm) long, taking them from the first third of the first joint of the straw. (You may either cut these pieces from straws of equal diameter or sort the cut pieces from largest to smallest in diameter and use the largest ones first.)

Hold the straw-covered wire core in a vertical position and set one of the 4"-long straws on top of it at a 45-degree angle, with the center of the short straw 3" (7.6 cm) from the bottom end of the core. Referring to Figure 6, wrap the right-hand portion of the straw under and around the core.

King Arthur's Wain

In early Celtic mythology, the constellation we know as the Big Dipper (or Ursa Major) was called Arthur's Wain or Arthur's Star. Thought to be the wagon that whisked the dying King to Avalon, the constellation was viewed as a sign that the King would someday return.

The circle in this weaving represents a wheel of the wagon, and the complete design suggests a star. The wonderful symmetry of the piece will enhance your plaiting collection and give you a great deal of enjoyment in the process.

The five arms of the star are created with a modified Glory Braid. Take care to be exact with the measurements of these arms. If one is even slightly larger than another, the effects will be noticeable in the finished project.

Instructions on following page

Challenge Rating

Time Rating

MATERIALS

110 long, large-diameter straws with large heads
(Black bearded wheat recommended)
Arms of star

Brass hoop, 14" (35.6 cm) in diameter
Braid-covered hoop

27 long straws without heads
Braid-covered hoop

TECHNIQUES

Glory Braid (pages 90-91)

Welsh Harp (pages 60-61)

Three-Straw Hair Braid (pages 28-29)

Adding new straws to Hair Braids (page 63)

Braid-covered hoop (page 69)

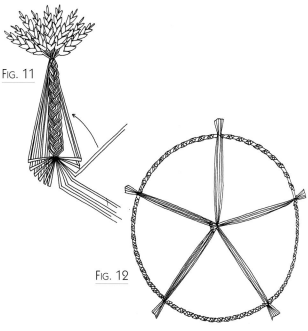

FIG. 11

FIG. 12

Tie together twelve very long straws and weave a Glory Braid 4" (10.2 cm) long. Tie the twelve straws off at the end of the plait. Place the plait on the work surface and spread the remaining straws out flat with the straws nearly side by side.

The next step is one you learned when making the Welsh Harp. Place a straightedge or ruler across the straws and perpendicular to them and 1-1/2" (3.8 cm) down from the tie. Bend the straw ends back over the ruler to make creases in each one. Lift the straws up and pinch the creases to make them sharp.

Bring the end of the outermost left-hand straw back to the starting point of the braid, at its back. Note that it should

form a 90-degree angle at the crease. Now move the straw next to it in a similar fashion, under the outermost straw, to bring its end to the back of the braid's starting point. The angle of its crease should be slightly less than 90 degrees.

Continue by folding the ends of all the left-hand straws back to the starting point, decreasing the angle at the crease of each one. Tie the six straws to the starting point of the plait and trim the tied straws close to the knot.

Next, fold the right-hand straws, working from the outermost straw inward and matching the straw positions with those of the straws in the left-hand group (Fig. 11). When you're finished, tie this group of six straws off at the starting point, too, and trim them close to the knot.

Repeat to make four more modified Glory Braids.

The brass hoop in this project is wrapped with a braid, just as the Alchemy hoop was wrapped (see page 69). Start by weaving a 60" (152.4 cm) length of Three-Straw Hair Braid, inserting news straws as necessary and testing the length of the braid before tying it off. (You'll probably need to add about four sets of inserts, but if you use small-diameter straws and place the wraps very close to each other, you may need more.) Remember not to trim the ends of the inserted straws until you've wrapped the braid around the hoop. If you trim them first, they may come out when the braid is pulled tight as you wrap. Secure one end of the finished braid to the hoop, wrap the hoop tightly, and tie off.

To locate the positions on the hoop where the points of the stars should be attached, use a fabric measuring tape to measure the circumference of the hoop and divide it by five. Mark each spot by inserting a straight pin through the braid on the hoop.

Tie fifty straws together about 1" (2.5 cm) below the heads and cut off the heads. While holding the bundle by the 1" straw sections, position the straws vertically and pull them down perpendicular to the tie, dividing them into five groups of ten straws each. Press down firmly against the straws above the tie to make each group form a right angle in relation to the 1"-long trimmed ends.

Arrange the straws in the center of the brass ring and tie each group of ten straws at a pin-marked location on the hoop (Fig. 12). Each arm should be 7" (17.8 cm) long. Trim any straws that extend beyond the circumference of the hoop.

To attach the modified Glory Braids to the five-armed straw core, first turn the hoop over. Then tie the starting point of each braid on top of a core arm at the point at which the arm is attached to the hoop. Also tie the ending point of each plait to the core straws at the tip of the Glory Braid.

Shield of the Winds III

The symbols in many wheat weavings are derived from beliefs surrounding the elements of nature so critical to the cultivation of grain: the harvest itself, the seasons, the sun, and the winds that pollinate or bring rain. In some places, straw shields were placed on barns to protect farm animals from danger, but the shield in the project presented here is intended to protect crops from the wind—no matter which direction it blows from.

Instructions on following page

This design, my third version of the Shield, is quite complex, but if you've practiced by making several of the previous projects in this book, you shouldn't have any trouble. Completing the beautiful design will certainly leave you with a great sense of accomplishment!

When weaving the Batwing circles, avoid using a smaller-diameter wheat variety such as a Plains bread wheat, as the shorter straws may make it necessary to readjust not only the numbers of new straws needed to make these plaits, but the measurements of various project parts as well. Black bearded wheat will work best.

FIG. 13

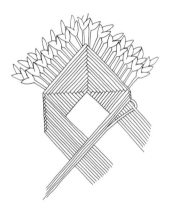

FIG. 14

MATERIALS

88 long, large-diameter straws with large heads
Corizons with arms (four)

2 pieces of medium-gauge wire, each 6-1/2" (16.5 cm) long
God's Eyes (four)

2 large-diameter straws without heads, each 6-1/2" long
God's Eyes (four)

4 pieces of medium-gauge wire, each 3" (7.6 cm) long
God's Eyes (four)

4 large-diameter straws without heads, each 3" long
God's Eyes (four)

80 long straws without heads
God's Eyes (four)

36 long, large-diameter straws without heads
Batwing circle (small)

54 long, large-diameter straws without heads
Batwing circle (large)

TECHNIQUES

Corizon (pages 64-65)

God's Eye (page 75)

Batwing (page 47)

Adding new straws to Batwings (page 76)

Each of the four Corizon plaits on the arms of the Shield contains 22 very long straws with heads. Start by making four Corizon plaits in the usual manner, but don't tie them off. Instead, determine which surface of each one looks best and turn that surface face up. Note that the loose straw—the last one added—will be on the left no matter which surface you choose to display. Lock this loose straw by lifting the second straw from the outside of the left-hand group and passing the outermost straw under it to rest at the inside of the right-hand group. Return the lifted straw to the work surface. Repeat this manipulation to pass all the left-hand straws over to the right. (Note that the last straw in this group will not have a straw under which to pass. Just crease the straw with your fingernail and bend it over itself to the opposite side.)

Now pass all the right-hand straws to the left in the same fashion (Fig. 13). Tie the two groups together, right underneath their point of intersection. Repeat to make three more arms in the same manner, striving to keep them the same in size and appearance. Trim the unwoven straw ends of each Corizon to 10-1/2" (26.7 cm) in length, measuring from the tie at the base of the design. Then tie two arms together as shown in Figure 14, with a Corizon facing up at each end.

The distance between the ties should be 10" (25.4 cm). Trim the excess straws very close to the knots.

Before tying the remaining two arms together, study Figure 15. Slip the straw ends of a single arm between the straws of the previously tied pair. Place the other single arm on top of the pair as shown. Position the arms on your work surface as if they were a plus sign and check to see that they're equal in length and exactly centered. Using heavy-duty carpet or linen thread, tie them together at their intersection point. Also tie the ends of the single arms together, just under the Corizons.

In the center of this project are four God's Eyes woven on two arms. To make each arm, first insert a 6-1/2" (16.5 cm) length of wire into a 6-1/2"-long straw and a 3"-long (7.6 cm) wire into a 3"-long straw. Then, using a scaffold knot, tie the two straw-covered wires together, locating the shorter core perpendicular to the longer core and 1-3/4" (4.4 cm) from one of its ends.

Around the tied cores, weave a God's Eye that measures 3" from tip to tip and tie it off. At the opposite end of the longer core, tie another straw-covered 3"-long wire, again 1-3/4" from the end (Fig. 16). Create a second God's Eye as before and tie it off. The two God's Eyes should meet in the middle of the longer straw-covered wire, and about 1/4" (6 mm) of straw-covered wire should protrude at each end.

Repeat to make another arm with two God's Eyes on it. If the God's Eyes don't meet or meet but don't measure exactly 3", make adjustments by weaving additional rows or unwrapping rows as necessary.

Tie the first set of God's Eyes to the center of the arms of the Shield, as shown in Figure 17. The two God's Eyes should cover a 6"-long (15.2 cm) portion of the 10"-long (25.4 cm) arms. Using the photo as a guide, bend two tips of each God's Eye up at 45-degree angles to create a concave front surface on each one.

Position the other pair of God's Eyes at right angles to the first set and tie this pair into place on the second arm of the shield. Bend the tips of this pair as before.

The two circles on the shield are made with Batwing plaits. Weave one plait approximately 24" (61.0 cm) long and one 36" (91.4 cm) long. If you're using large-diameter straws for these plaits, you'll probably need to insert three complete sets of new straws into the shorter braid and five complete sets into the longer one. Plan ahead and soak plenty of additional straws so that you don't find yourself short in the middle of making the project.

Arrange the shorter Batwing to form a circle around the God's Eyes, with the batwing tips on its inside edge. Check to see that it fits properly, making minor adjustments to its length as necessary. (If there are no gaps in the plait, you may stretch it slightly.) Tie the ends of the plait together. Then stitch the circle to the arms by running the sewing needle from back to front, up through the arm and plait and back down again through the

plait and arm so that you can tie the knot underneath the arm.

Arrange the larger circle to hide the areas where the end of one arm meets the Corizon on the other. (Note that the tied arm straws are on top of the arms in two of the four locations.) Stitch the larger circle in place with a needle and thread as before.

Before drying the completed piece, fan out the heads of each Corizon and make sure that both the top and bottom surfaces of the shield are exposed to the air. Placing the project on a screen will ensure adequate air circulation.

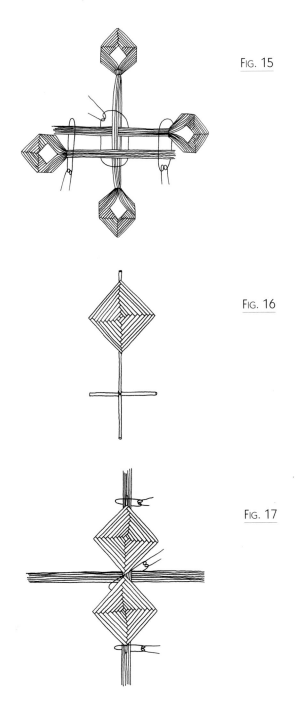

FIG. 15

FIG. 16

FIG. 17

115

MATERIALS

18 long, large-diameter straws without heads
  Arms

7 large-diameter straws with large heads
  Hair

26 long, large-diameter straws with large heads
  Figure and head

8 straws with large heads
  Love Knots (arms)

72 large-diameter straws
  Love Knots (arms)

9 large-diameter straws without heads
  Cross pieces

4 straws with large heads
  Love Knots (base)

TECHNIQUES

Luton Railroad (pages 29-30)

Four-Straw FTG (pages 30-31)

Love Knots (page 73)

Three-Straw Hair Braid (pages 28-29)

Two Straws at Four Corners (page 36)

The Gleaner

The gleaner, who was usually a woman, walked the fields and picked up the grain that remained after the regular reaping. Wheat-woven female figures such as the one in this design were ancient symbols of the bountiful harvest. Christine Gilbreath has created this stunning figure in keeping with the harvest tradition. Black bearded wheat is highly recommended for this project

The two braids that make up the arms should be woven so that their patterns will be opposed in the finished project. First weave a 4" (10.2 cm) length of Luton Railroad, making the starting tie 1/2" (1.3 cm) below the tips of the straws and arranging seven straws on the right and two on the left. Don't tie the straws off when you're finished. Make another 4"-long Luton Railroad, but start this one with two straws on the right and seven on the left. After making both braids, lock all of the straws on each one toward the side with two straws. Tie the braids off 1/2" from the ends of the plaited sections (Fig. 18).

To join the unwoven ends of the arms, first fold the unwoven straws of each one downward at a right angle.

FIG. 18

Then tie the arms together over the ties at their ends and again 2" (5.1 cm) from that point. Trim the straws about 1/2" (1.3 cm) beyond the tie. The 2"-long core of tied straws will serve as a body core and will provide stability and fullness to the figure.

To create the figure's hair, tie together seven straws, about 1" (2.5 cm) below their large heads. (Tie firmly, but don't crush the straws.)

Next, form the figure by tying 26 large-headed straws together, 10" (25.4 cm) below the straw heads. To make the head, turn the straws so that the heads face you and trim the ends above the 10" tie into a head shape). Turn the figure face down and tie the hair straws to it at the back of the neck (Fig. 19). To hide this tie, pull up one of the longest hair straws from under the knot, wrap it around the neck, and secure it to the back of the neck with thread.

Divide the figure straws in half (from front to back) and insert the arms, pushing them up as far as they will go. Tie the figure straws together 2" (5.1 cm) below this point (Fig. 20). Cover the tie at the waist by wrapping it with another hair straw and securing the straw in back, just as you did at the neck. Trim the five remaining hair straws just below the waist.

Next, tie the arms together at the starting points of the plaits, shaping them as shown in Figure 21.

To make the sheaf of grain in the Gleaner's arms, weave two Four-Straw FTG plaits, each 4" to 5" (10.2 to 12.7 cm). Tie each plait into a traditional Love Knot. Arrange the Knots in the arms and tie them to the arms with thread. Then feed the untrimmed thread ends from the Love Knots around to the back of the body, just below the waist, and tie them securely to hold the arms in place.

The divided oval pattern at the base of the figure is made with three 11"-long (27.9 cm) Three-Straw Hair Braids. After making these plaits, weave one of them through the 13 pairs of body straws, as shown in Figure 21. Repeat with a second Hair Braid, but this time, pass the braid over the straws that you previously went under and under those you passed over. Repeat with the third braid, weaving this braid just as you did the first. Now shape the top and bottom braids to form an oval. Tie all three braids together at both ends and trim their excess straws about 1/4" to 1/2" (6 to 13 mm) from each knot.

To make the small Love Knots that embellish the base of the figure, first weave a pair of Two Straws at Four Corners plaits, each approximately 4" (10.2 cm) long. Tie each plait into a Love Knot and tie one at each side of the braided oval.

Make sure that the body straws rest flat before setting the completed project out to dry.

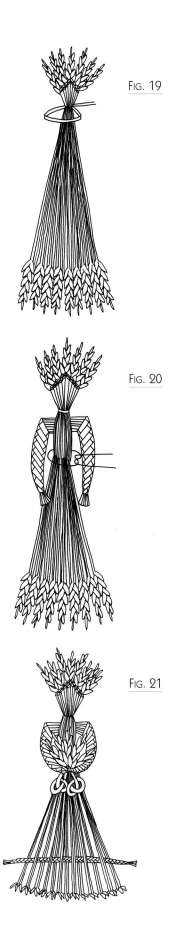

FIG. 19

FIG. 20

FIG. 21

8

International Designs

A rt forms that have accompanied the harvests of different cultures bear interesting similarities, and wheat weaving is no exception. The same patterns have appeared worldwide and although they bear different names, they often arose from similar harvest beliefs and customs. In Europe, these shared designs can be explained by the migration of peoples from one area to another, but similar wheat-weaving designs appear in separate continents as well. House Blessings with their wheat heads fanned out, for example, are common around the world, as are weavings symbolizing love and fertility.

Cultural "markers" distinguish the wheat weavings of one area from those of another. Wheat-woven Lithuanian songbirds are unique to the Baltic. St. Brigit's Crosses from Ireland and dolls from Russia are like wheat weavings from no other country. In this chapter you'll learn how to make a few representative designs from around the world.

Polish Crown

Wheat-woven crowns are often associated with the end of the harvest. In most cultures, bringing in the last of the grain was viewed as the successful culmination of an entire year's work and was therefore celebrated with much ceremony and revelry.

The crown designs that survive today may be relics of the traditional custom—in many cultures—of weaving a crown for the queen of the harvest. These designs may also represent the crowning achievement of having completed the harvest itself. The project presented here is similar to the wheat-woven crowns made in Poland.

Time Rating

FIG. 1

MATERIALS

5 long, large-diameter straws without heads
Upper base (Compass Weave)

1 piece of medium-gauge wire, 3-1/2" (8.9 cm) long
Upper base (Compass Weave)

10 long, large-diameter straws without heads
Lower base (Ten-Straw Diamond)

21 long, large-diameter straws without heads
Three-loop center section

16 long straws with heads
Upper crown (inside)

8 long straws with heads
Upper crown (outside)

7 short straws with large heads
Column

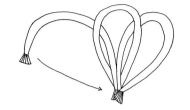

FIG. 2

TECHNIQUES

Compass Weave (pages 32-33)

Ten-Straw Diamond (page 40)

Seven-Straw FTG (page 32)

Expanded Rustic (page 44)

Stretched Four-Straw FTG (pages 30-31)

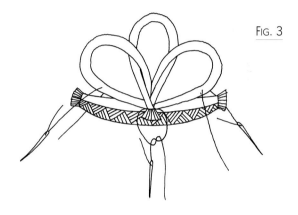

FIG. 3

To make the upper section of the base, start by covering a 3-1/2"-long (8.9 cm) wire with a straw. Tie four straws 1/4" (6 mm) from one end and weave a 3"-long (7.6 cm) Compass Weave plait. Tie the plait off so that 1/4" of the core extends at the end.

To make the lower section of the base, tie ten straws together and weave a 3"-long Ten-Straw Diamond plait. Fasten the two sections of the base together by tying the two plaits together as shown in Figure 1, positioning the Compass Weave plait to cover just a bit of the upper edge of the Diamond plait. Set the base aside.

The three-loop center of the crown is made with three 6"-long (15.2 cm) Seven-Straw FTG plaits. Weave the first one and tie its ends together to make a loop. Weave the other two and interlock the three plaits as shown in Figure 2, tying the ends of the last two plaits together so that they rest side by side on top of the first plait.

Before making the other sections of this project, you must tie together the base and three-loop center section. Turn the base onto its face and position the center section as shown in Figure 3. Run a needle and thread through the base of the loops, inserting the needle so that the thread won't show at the front of the tied loops. Then tie the thread ends securely.

Pull down each side loop so that its bottom edge meets the upper edge of the Compass Weave plait. Using a needle again, run thread through the bottom edge of each loop and around the base. Tie the thread ends securely.

Two 6"-long (15.2 cm) Expanded Rustic plaits run from the top of the design to its base, to form the inside of the crown. Weave each plait, tie it off, and set it aside.

The outermost plaits of the crown are 9"-long (22.9 cm) stretched Four-Straw FTG plaits. Weave and tie off two of these, trimming the straws and threads close to the knots. Set the plaits aside for the moment.

FIG. 4

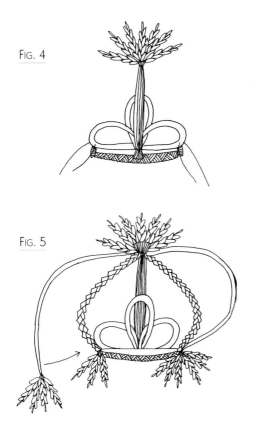

FIG. 5

To make the vertical column for the crown, tie seven straws together near the heads and again 4-1/4" (10.8 cm) down from the first tie. Trim the remaining straws at the end.

To assemble the various sections, start by attaching the column to the back of the crown's base, placing the thread over the bottom tie on the column and the tie that joins the three loops (Fig. 4).

Next, turn the base and column over, front face up. Tie the ends of the Expanded Rustic plaits to the sides of the column at its top. Then trim their straw ends 1" (2.5 cm) above the knot. Arrange these plaits to form the inner crown shape shown in Figure 5 and tie their other ends to the ends of the two-part base.

Turn the assembled sections face down and tie the ends of the stretched Four-Straw FTG plaits to the top of the column, at its back. Turn the project face up and tie the other ends of these stretched plaits on top of the ends of the base. Pull the heads of the stretched plaits down to cover the heads of the Expanded Rustic plaits.

If you like, you may hide the thread at the top of the column by wrapping one of the 1" (2.5 cm) lengths of straw from an Expanded Rustic plait around it. Tie the straw to the back of the design.

The Eye of the Moon: A Moroccan God's Eye

The God's Eye, which we tend to associate with Mexico, was probably brought to the New World by the armies of Cortez, as the design was also made in Spain and by the Moors of northern Africa.

We don't know much about the original Eye of the Moon or its symbolic meanings. It's possible that the straw tassels may have represented moonbeams, or perhaps they were added to emphasize the ceremonial appearance of the piece. Tassels did represent womanhood and may have served as symbolic protection for females. Both old and contemporary examples have been made with multi-colored straws, creating a panorama of texture and tone.

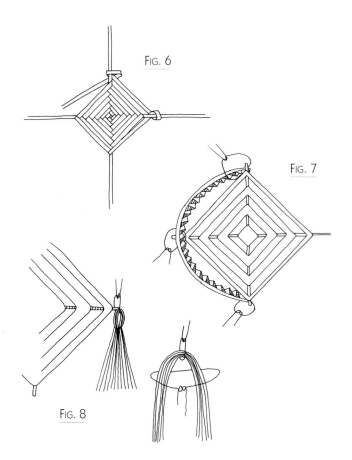

FIG. 6

FIG. 7

FIG. 8

Challenge Rating

Time Rating

MATERIALS

27 long straws without heads
    God's Eye

2 pieces of heavy-gauge wire, each 7" (17.8 cm) long
    God's Eye

20 long, large-diameter straws without heads
    Tassels

27 long, large-diameter straws without heads
    Crescent

TECHNIQUES

God's Eye (page 75)

Batwing (page 47)

To make the two-piece core, use a scaffold knot to tie two 7"-long (17.8 cm) pieces of heavy-gauge wire together in a plus-sign shape. Begin the God's Eye in the usual manner, using your smallest straws first. Complete six rows on each of the four sides of the core. Then, rather than placing the straw on top of the wire core and wrapping down and around, position the straw under the wire and wrap it up and around, going in the opposite direction (Fig. 6). This will cause subsequent rows to be woven on the other surface of the plait.

After reversing the manipulation in this fashion, turn the God's Eye over and work its back as if it were the top, making six more rows on each of the four sides. Then bring the straw underneath the wire core. Wrap it up and around again to bring the weave to the opposite surface of the God's Eye again. Turn the plait over again and continue to create more rows.

Continue weaving in this manner, switching surfaces after each six rows, until you have three sets of six rows worked on each surface. (The final set of six will be woven on the back.) Reverse the plait once more and create a border of two more rows on the front surface. Tie the final straw to the wire core and trim the ends of the wires to about 1/2" (1.3 cm) beyond the corners of the plait. Set this piece aside for now.

The crescent is made with a 13"-long (33.0 cm) Batwing plait. Weave this length, using a total of 27 straws (9 to start and 2 sets of inserts). Shape the finished Batwing into a semicircle and tie it to the top, left, and bottom corners of the God's Eye (Fig. 7).

To make each tassel, first bunch together ten large-diameter straws. Trim both ends of the straws to leave a 9"-long (22.9 cm) bundle taken from their centers. Using a craft knife, ribbon shredder, or straw splitter, split each straw into splits as narrow as possible. Tie the bundle of splits together in the middle and fold them at the tie, leaving the thread ends untrimmed. Tie once again 1/2" (1.3 cm) from the top (Fig. 8) and trim the split ends to 4" (10.2 cm) in length. Repeat to make a second tassel. Using the untrimmed threads, tie one tassel to the bottom of the diamond pattern and one to the right corner. Fan out the ends of the split straws. Most tassels curl a bit as they dry, lending them texture and form.

St. Brigit's Cross

Legend has it that this traditional wheat weaving from Ireland was first made by Brigit—a patron saint of that country— when she was imprisoned for her faith. Although the original design may well have been made with rushes, wheat versions have been recreated for centuries. Some folklorists believe that the design— also known as a market-place cross— was placed at road intersections to indicate to people who couldn't read that a market fair would be held at that spot.

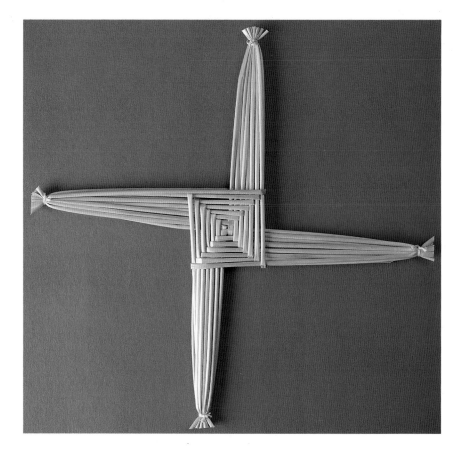

MATERIALS

28 long, large-diameter straws without heads
    Entire piece

TECHNIQUES

St. Brigit's Cross (see this section)

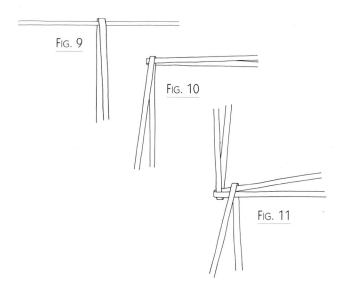

FIG. 9

FIG. 10

FIG. 11

Challenge Rating   Time Rating

Make the core first by positioning two straws to make a plus sign, placing the horizontal straw on top. Pull the upper section of the vertical straw down on top of its other half (Fig. 9). Turn the weave 90 degrees counterclockwise. Repeat to fold down the straw that is now vertical (Fig. 10).

Turn the straws 90 degrees counterclockwise again. Add the next straw by placing it to the right of the vertical folded straw and under the horizontal folded straw, as shown in Figure 11. Fold the added straw, turn the straws once again, and add the fourth and final straw of this round in the same fashion.

Continue to add and fold straws. Avoid letting them bunch up or lie on top of those in a previous round. Instead, build the weave outward, resting the straws side by side. At first, you may find it difficult to hold the arms together and at right angles, but as the weave gains substance, this will prove easier. Just remember to watch for gaps and fill them by repositioning and tightening the straws as necessary.

When all 28 straws have been incorporated, tie each arm off about 4" (10.2 cm) from the center of the design. Trim the ends of the straws and threads.

Circle of Spring: A Czech Bouquet

The Czech people love their national flowers—daisies, cornflowers, and poppies—as well as wheat. Marian Vauvra has designed this Circle of Spring, which combines appliqué and woven elements, as a reminder of the coming of this season and its flowers.

The light-colored appliqué sections may be made with oat splits if you wish.

Challenge Rating

Time Rating

MATERIALS

50 long, large-diameter straws
Appliqué splits

9 long straws without heads
Long curled plaits (three)

18 long straws without heads
Short curled plaits (six)

18 long straws without heads
Looped plaits (three)

2 damp straw splits
Rose

3 heads of beardless wheat, straws removed
Embellishment

TECHNIQUES

Appliqué (see pages 21-22 and this section)

Catfoot (page 35)

Six-Straw FTG (page 31)

Split straw roses (page 139)

Using tracing paper and a pencil or a sheet of clear plastic and a felt-tip pen, trace three each of the flower-part patterns and one of the circle pattern provided in Figure 12 on page 126. (The pens made for use with overhead projectors work well on plastic.) Transfer the traced patterns to a manila folder or card stock that is similar in color to wheat and cut out each one.

After reviewing the section on straw splits in Chapter 2, prepare 50 splits that are as flat, long, and wide as possible. Separate the darker splits from the lighter ones so that you can select from each batch to enhance the appearance of the completed piece.

Spread a thin, even layer of craft glue on the bottom half of pattern #1. Place several of the darkest straw splits horizontally across the bottom of this pattern, making sure to position each one right next to the previous one. Using your burnishing tool, press the splits firmly into the glue. This will help hold them in place. Rub off any excess glue with a dry cloth or your finger. Repeat to cover the rest of the pattern with splits. Turn the pattern over and trim any overhanging split ends from it. (Whenever possible, use these trimmed splits instead of new splits to cover the other patterns.) Now repeat to cover the other two patterns #1 with splits.

Fig. 12

Select several light-colored splits for tulip pattern #2. Apply the splits to this pattern as you did before, but position them diagonally. Trim the ends and then apply splits to the other two identical shapes.

Again select some of the dark splits and cover the three tulip patterns #3, positioning these splits vertically. Burnish and trim as before.

The three poppies are made in the same manner. Use light-colored splits on pattern #4, arranging them vertically; medium-hued splits on pattern #5, arranging them diagonally; and dark splits on pattern #6, arranging them horizontally.

Cover the circle pattern with splits as well. Then use a needle or pin to poke two holes in the circle, about 1/2" (1.3 cm) from its edge, and run a short length of fine-gauge wire through the holes to make a hanger.

Next, weave three Catfoot plaits, each 4-1/2" (11.4 cm) long and six more, each 2-3/4" (7.0 cm) long. Using Figure 13 as a guide, curl each longer braid around itself three times and tie the ends together as shown. Curl each shorter braid around itself twice and tie off as well. Set the curled plaits aside to dry.

To make the larger loops around the center of the design, weave three Six-Straw FTG plaits, each 2-1/4" (5.7 cm) long, and tie their ends together to make three elongated loops.

To make the straw rose for the center of the design, follow the instructions on page 139.

Assembly of this project is straightforward. Pin the circle temporarily to a piece of cardboard or rigid polystyrene foam. Glue the tulips and then the poppies to the split-covered circle, as shown in Figure 14 and the photo. Trim any parts that seem out of place. As you arrange these parts for

Fig. 13

Fig. 14

Lithuanian Songbird

Lithuanians have traditionally given straw sodas (or trees of life) to newly married couples in order to bless their union with abundance. The word "soda" means orchard and reflects the importance that farming and gardening have had in this Baltic country.

Trees of life are always geometric in shape. Large or small (depending upon the expertise of the maker and importance of the occasion), each soda contains a gardener, birds, flowers, stars, and many more symbolic shapes.

gluing, remember that the hanger must be at the 12 o'clock position, immediately behind one of the tulips.

Next, glue three wheat heads in place (if you don't have beardless wheat, trim the beards first) on top of the tulip stems. Using the photo as a placement guide, arrange a loop of Six-Straw FTG plait on top of each wheat head, gluing its tip to the circle. Glue the six smaller curls between the wheat heads, in pairs, at the base of each poppy. Glue the larger curls above and between the pairs of smaller curls. Finally, glue the rose to the center of the design.

Instructions on following pages

The songbirds that are usually attached to larger sodas have become so popular that they're often made as independent designs and are sometimes called sodas themselves. In parts of Lithuania, the birds are hung by closed windows to test for drafts before winter arrives. If they flutter in the summer breeze, the window is repaired. Larger songbirds are made at Easter and decorated eggs are cradled within them as symbols of spring and rebirth.

Creating these delicate and wispy straw birds, which make lovely gifts and Christmas ornaments, isn't as easy as you might think at first glance, but patience will bring success. Start by preparing the splits of straw. The wider and longer the splits, the bigger your bird will be.

Challenge Rating

Time Rating

MATERIALS

2 straw splits, each 1/8" x 15" (.3 x 38.1 cm)
Basket-weave body

12 straw splits, each 1/8" x 10-1/2" (.3 x 26.7 cm)
Basket-weave body

4 second-joint straws, each 1-1/2" (3.8 cm) long
Hanger

2 second-joint straws, each 3/4" (1.9 cm) long
Hanger

TECHNIQUES

(See this section)

Soak 14 large-diameter straws. Then split and cut them to the dimensions indicated in the "Materials" list, trimming the length and width of each one. Turn the splits starch side up and de-pith.

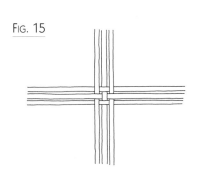

Fig. 15

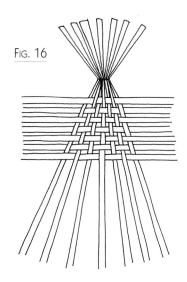

Fig. 16

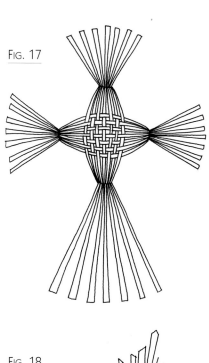

Fig. 17

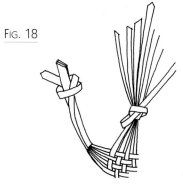

Fig. 18

Re-soak the splits for about four hours, adding 1 part vinegar to 5 parts water if yellowing is a problem for the wheat variety you're using. (Rinse the straws well if you've included vinegar.)

Because splits dry out very quickly, it's best to avoid making this project on a very hot, dry day or in an air-conditioned room. Keep the splits under a damp towel as you work. If you notice that the splits are still drying too quickly, keep a spray bottle filled with water nearby and use it as necessary.

To begin making the basket-weave body, first study Figure 15. Then place one 15"-long (38.1 cm) split on top of the other 15"-long split, with the intersection point at the upper third of each split. Slip two 10-1/2"-long (26.6 cm) splits under the horizontal split, arranging them on each side of the vertical split. Then add two 10-1/2"-long horizontal splits, above and below the horizontal straw, weaving them under, over, and under the vertical splits. Continue to add splits, weaving them in the same fashion, until all 12 have been incorporated.

To form the neck of the bird, tie off the splits as shown in Figure 16, but don't trim the thread ends. The body splits should now be fanned out into a V-shape. Pull these fanned splits together and tie them to form the tail (Fig. 17), but don't trim the thread ends. Note that the body will form a cup shape when this tie is made. Tie the left and right wings in the same fashion, leaving the excess thread lengths untrimmed.

To make the beak, first locate the 15"-long split among the tied neck splits. Then, referring to Figure 18, wrap this split around the other neck splits, about 3/4" (1.9 cm) from their ends, and slip the end of the split through the wrap to knot it. The end of the wrapped and knotted split should protrude to form the beak. Pull it tightly to tighten the wrap and secure the straws. Then trim the tied splits to shape the bird's head.

Now locate the 15"-long split in the wings and repeat to wrap its ends around the thread tie at the base of each wing. Pull the split ends to tighten the wraps and secure the straws. Trim the wing and tail splits.

To make the hanger, first cut a dry second-joint straw into a total of six sections: four sections, each 1" to 1-1/2" (2.5 to 3.8 cm) long; and two sections, each 3/4" (1.9 cm) long. String each of the untrimmed threads at the base of the neck, wings, and tail through the longer second-joint straw sections as if you were stringing beads. Tie the four threads together at the top of these second-joint straw sections. Doing this will pull the wing, head, and tail straws into position. The straws should form an equilateral pyramid shape.

Next, thread the four threads through the two 3/4"-long straws. Tie the gathered threads into a single knot just above these straws and use the thread ends to form a looped hanger.

Candle Glow Wreath

The candle is a worldwide welcoming symbol for friends. In fact, leaving a light burning for the safe return home of a loved one seems to be a universal theme, one which Donna Hall has depicted in this delightful straw wreath.

Instructions on following pages

Materials

1 piece of medium-gauge wire, 10" long (25.4 cm)
   Wreath core

1 medium-diameter straw without a head,
12-3/4" (32.4 cm) long
   Wreath core

60-75 long, small-diameter straws
   Wreath

3 small-diameter straws without heads
   Love Knot

6 small-diameter straws without heads
   Flower

8 small-diameter straws without heads
   Plaited bow

2 small-diameter straws without heads
   Hanger

Techniques

Four-Straw Spiral (page 50)

Two Straws at Three Corners (page 37)

Six-Straw Spiral (pages 50-51)

Appliqué (pages 21-22 and 125-126)

Rope Weave (page 34)

Increasing a Spiral (see this section)

To make the core for the circular wreath, cover a 10"-long (25.4 cm) piece of medium-gauge wire with a 12-3/4"-long (32.4 cm) straw, leaving a 1-3/8" (3.5 cm) straw overlap at each end. Tie two to three small-diameter straws to the straw-covered wire.

Align the ends of four very delicate working straws with the ends of the core straws. Then tie these working straws to the core straws, 1-3/8" up from their ends so that the tie will cover a wire-filled rather than a hollow section of the core straw. Do not trim the thread ends. You should now have five 1-3/8" straw lengths beneath the tie.

Weave a 10"-long Four-Straw Spiral plait, inserting new straws as necessary to create an even plait of the correct length. Tie the plait off at the other end of the core straw, over the wire within it. Trim the remaining straw lengths to 1-3/8", but don't trim the thread ends.

Bend the plait into a round shape, molding it around a cylindrical object such as a glass. Tie the two plait ends together, but leave the thread ends untrimmed. Bend the two sets of 1-3/8" straw lengths at each end so that they flare out at right angles to each other. Trim these straws at angles and set the wreath aside to dry.

To make the candle flame, split and iron flat about 1" (2.5 cm) at one end of a very large-diameter straw. Then, using Figure 19 as a guide, add two straws to the candle-flame straw, tying them beneath the flame and again 1-1/2" (3.8 cm) beneath the first tie. These will serve as a core. Very carefully, trim their ends at the bottom of the flame end.

Position five working straws around the flame, and tie them just beneath it. Using scissors, carefully trim these straws without damaging the rounded portion of the flame straw or the two core straws, underneath the tie and as close to it as possible.

Turn the tied straws around so that the flame is at the bottom, and use the working straws to weave a Five-Straw Spiral plait, 1-1/2" long. (Note that you'll be weaving away from the flame.) Tie the plait off, but don't trim the working or flame straws.

In the finished project, three decorations rest at the sides of the candle. To make the first—a Love Knot—start by plaiting a 3-1/2"-long (8.9 cm) Two Straws at Three Corners plait. Tie off its ends (leave the thread ends untrimmed) and set this favor aside to dry.

The flower is made by "opening a Spiral"—gradually increasing its width as you weave its length. Start by reviewing the "Spiral Plaits" section, paying special attention to Figure 95 on page 49. As you can see in this illustration, normal Spirals are woven by placing the working straw (in this case straw E) directly on top of the corner to which it moves (the corner at straw B).

To open a Spiral, you position the working straw just slightly to the outside of the corner to which it moves instead of on top of it. As you continue to weave, the Spiral will therefore expand in width. To make this flower, tie together six straws and weave a 1"-wide (2.5 cm) Spiral plait, opening it as described. Tie the plait off and set it aside for now.

To make the appliqué leaf, start by tracing the pattern shown in Figure 20, transferring it to a manila folder or buff-colored card stock, and cutting out the paper shape. Draw a curved line down the length of the paper shape to divide the leaf in half. Completely cover one half with craft glue. Place a split on the pattern at the angle indicated in Figure 20, positioning it just at the edge of the curved line. Trim away the split that extends beyond the pattern. Position this section of trimmed split next to the applied split to cover another portion of the leaf. Continue to cover the straw by applying trimmed sections of split to cover this half of the leaf. Before covering the other half of the leaf, carefully run the blade of your craft knife down the curved center line to trim away any split ends that extend beyond it. Take care not to slice the paper! Now repeat to cover the other half of the leaf with splits.

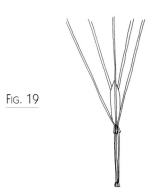

FIG. 19

To make the plaited bow at the base of the project, align four straws side by side and tie a knot in them (using the straws themselves, not thread) about 1" (2.5 cm) from their ends. Separate the straws into two groups of two straws each and plait a 3-1/2" to 4" (8.9 to 10.2 cm) length of Rope Weave, adding a set of four straws as you weave to complete the necessary length. To add straws to a Rope Weave, rest the thicker end of the new straw on top of the left-hand group, twist it in, and pass the group to the right. In order to space the new inserts correctly, add each one only after making a few twist-and-switch manipulations with the last. Make sure that you have at least 2" (5.1 cm) of remaining straw lengths when the plait is finished. Tie these lengths into a knot just at the end of the weave, and trim the straws to 1" (2.5 cm) in length. Arrange the plait into two loops, as shown in the photo and tie the bow loosely with thread. Trim the thread ends and set the bow aside for now.

FIG. 20

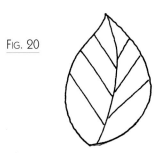

The extremely narrow hanger consists of a 4-1/2"-long (11.4 cm) two-straw Rope Weave, which, even though it contains only one straw in each "group," is made in the same fashion as any other Rope Weave. As you twist each individual straw, you'll notice that it tightens and shrinks. Tie the weave off when you're finished, leaving the thread ends untrimmed.

FIG. 21

Start assembling the project by using the untrimmed thread ends on the wreath to tie the candle to its back. Then, referring to Figure 21, use a needle and thread to stitch the spiral flower to the candle and wreath. Glue the leaf to the back of the flower and wreath. Stitch the Love Knot to the back of the candle, using a needle and the untrimmed thread ends on the Knot. Use the untrimmed thread ends on the hanger to stitch the hanger to the top back of the wreath, taking care to run the thread through the edge of the spiral and around the wire core as you do; the thread shouldn't show at the front of the wreath. Finally, use a short length of raffia to tie the bow into place at the base of the wreath and in front of it; the raffia will hide the original thread tie on the bow.

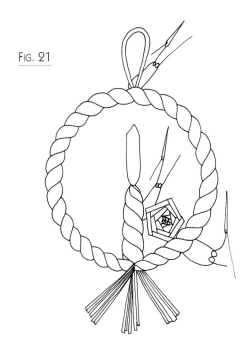

Irish Claedagh

Challenge Rating

Time Rating

One of the most famous surviving heart designs—which was often incorporated into wedding rings—is the Irish Claedagh from the city of Claedagh in Galway County, Ireland. The same design—in straw—has been recreated by several generations of Claedagh's wheat weavers. This is our version; we hope you'll like it.

MATERIALS

20 long, large-diameter straws with large heads
Heart with column

12 straws for splits
Crown

8 small-diameter straws without heads
Border of crown

6 small-diameter straws without heads
Loops at crown peak

15 to 25 straws without heads
Core for Spiral

28 to 36 long straws without heads
Spiral

14 straws without heads
Cuffs

TECHNIQUES

Ten-Straw Diamond (page 40)

Appliqué (pages 21-22 and 125-126)

Rustic (page 43)

Two Straws at Four Corners (page 36)

Love Knots (page 73)

Four-Straw Spiral (page 50)

Seven-Straw Ribbon (page 39)

To make the heart that is cradled by the hands, weave two 6-1/2"-long (16.5 cm) Ten-Straw Diamond plaits, tying them off at their ends. Tie their starting points together, shape them into a heart, being careful to display their flat surfaces, and tie their ending points together. Bring the remaining straw lengths from each arm down the center of the heart to form a column behind the point of the heart. Tie the joined starting points of the plaits to the upper surface of the base of the column and trim the remaining straw lengths beneath the tie.

Next, trace all the patterns—including the hands—in Figure 22 and transfer them to a manila folder or to card stock. (You'll need two diamond shapes.) Cut out the paper shapes. Draw a vertical line on the crown-base pattern to divide the pattern in half. Cover the right half with craft glue and then with splits, positioning the splits at acute angles, as shown in the photo at left. Allow each split to extend just slightly over the center line.

Turn the crown base face down and, using scissors, trim the splits at its edge. Turn the crown face up, position a ruler over the splits on the vertical dividing line, and cut away the edges of the splits to the left of this line. (Be careful not to slice the paper beneath.)

Repeat to cover the left half of the crown. Trim as before. Glue two splits over the center line where the other splits meet at the center of the crown. Then use a burnishing tool to rub the upper surfaces of the splits.

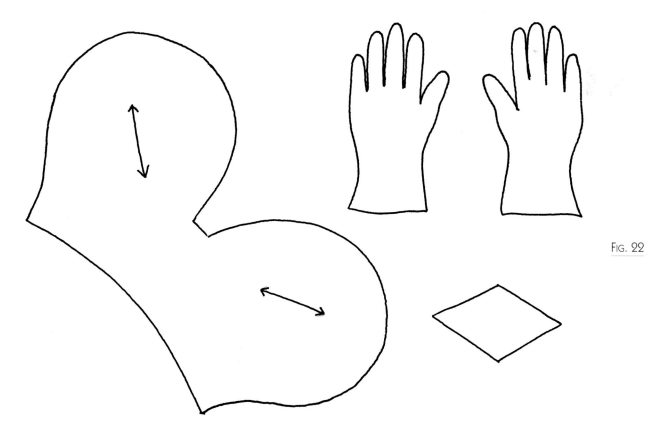

FIG. 22

Next, cover the two diamond shapes and the hands with splits, positioning the splits as shown in the photo. Apply glue to the backs of the diamonds and press them into place on the crown base. Set the hands aside.

To make the decorative plait that borders the crown, first weave two 5-1/2"-long (36.0 cm) Four-Straw Rustic plaits. These plaits must be shaped and dried before they're attached to the crown, or the moisture in them will curl the splits. To guarantee that the plaits dry to the correct shape, trace the crown pattern onto a sheet of cardboard and pin the plaits to the cardboard over the traced lines.

When the plaits have dried, glue them to the edges of the crown with hot-melt glue. (If you'd rather use craft glue, just be sure to pin the plaits in place as the glue dries.) No matter which glue you use, apply it a bit at a time, pressing down only a short portion of the plait before gluing down the next portion.

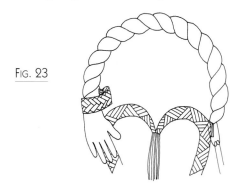
FIG. 23

The woven embellishment at the peak of the crown consists of two Love Knots made with two 3" (15.2 cm) lengths of Two Straws at Four Corners plait and a single 3"-length of the same plait, shaped into a loop. After weaving all three plaits, shape two into Love Knots and glue them to the back of the crown, arranging their inner loops to form a heart shape. Then shape the larger plait into a loop and glue it over the Love Knots.

The arms that hold the heart consist of a 16" (40.6 cm) length of Four-Straw Spiral plait woven around a 1/2"-diameter (1.3 cm) core made with 15 to 25 straws. (The number of straws will depend on the diameters of the straws available to you.) Weave this plait and tie off each end, but don't trim the thread ends.

Bend the Spiral plait into a circular shape, leaving it open at the bottom to accommodate the heart and hands. Allow this spiral section to dry. Then, using a needle and the untrimmed thread ends, stitch the spiral to the back of the heart (Fig. 23).

Glue the hands to the ends of the spiral, positioning them so that the thumbs and the ends of the fingers extend to touch the heart. Now make the cuffs by weaving two 3" (7.6 cm) lengths of Seven-Straw Ribbon plait, shaping them into circles, and allowing them to dry. Wrap the dried plaits around the ends of the spiral so that they cover the ends of the hands. Glue the ends of each cuff together to hold it in place. Glue the finger tips and thumb to the front surface of the heart. Finally, using the photo as a placement guide, glue the bottom tips of the crown underneath the top of the heart.

North African Cage

This project, which is quite easy to make, is known by many names, including African Fringe, Cage Fan, and Cage. Primitive and ancient in design, the Cage is still made in many parts of North Africa, especially in Egypt and Morocco, but is seldom woven for the tourist trade. In fact, if you were to seek it out, you would meet with much superstition and mistrust on the part of local weavers. Interestingly, its pattern suggests an association with the Welsh Fan and Corizon. Although the Cage isn't usually referred to as a House Blessing, its purpose was—and is—to bless the home.

MATERIALS

1 piece of heavy-gauge wire, 10" long
    Core

1 straw without head, 10" (25.4 cm) long
    Core

40 long straws with heads
    Cage

4 long straws with heads
    Hanger

TECHNIQUES

Straw-covered wires (page 33)

Four-Straw FTG (pages 30-31)

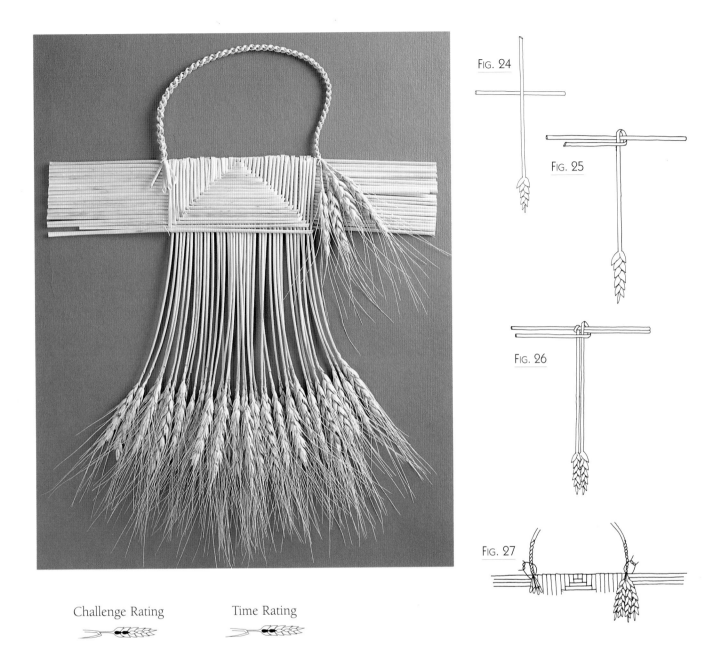

FIG. 24

FIG. 25

FIG. 26

FIG. 27

Challenge Rating

Time Rating

If you can't find 40 matched straws, use the ones with the largest heads first, incorporating those with the smallest heads last.

Insert the piece of wire into the 10"-long (25.4 cm) straw. Place this straw on the work surface and position a straw perpendicular to and on top of it, with the head about 6" (15.2 cm) below the core straw (Fig. 24). Bend the upper section of the straw on top as shown in Figure 25, wrapping it tightly around and to the left as you do.

Turn the weave over, holding the wrap securely in place. Add a new straw as shown in Figure 26, and repeat. Continue to add new straws (always on the right of the previous straws), turning the weave over each time, until all 40 straws have been incorporated. Tie the last straw to the previous round at the corner where the plait ends. Then trim the straw ends to the length of the core.

To make the hanger, weave a Four-Straw FTG plait. Tie off its ends, stretch the braid to at least 9" (22.9 cm) in length and tie it onto the core straw at the ends of the woven pattern (Fig. 27).

An easy variation of the North African Cage includes making a V-shape with the straw heads by raising every other head up very slightly as you add the 40 straws. You may also cut a pattern into the straws ends that extend from the woven pattern.

Straw Embellishments

C ompleted projects sometimes benefit from the addition of a small decorative element or two. Ribbons and bows are attractive and easy to add, of course, but embellishments made from straw add a special touch of their own. The small straw items that you'll learn how to make in this chapter will not only serve to add interest to your larger straw projects, but can serve as appealing additions to gift packages and Christmas trees as well.

Straw Bow

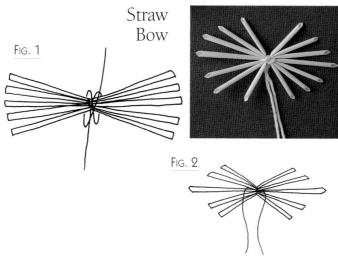

Fig. 1

Fig. 2

This delightful bow, which adorns the Osburn Crown on page 107, is very easy to make. Simply cut short lengths from the narrow ends of several straws. While holding the straws flat and side by side, wrap a length of thread around them (Fig. 1), but don't trim the thread ends yet. Trim the straws as shown in Fig. 2, and run both threads ends through the center straws so that when you tie the bow to your work, the straws will remain at a horizontal plane to it.

Straw Coil

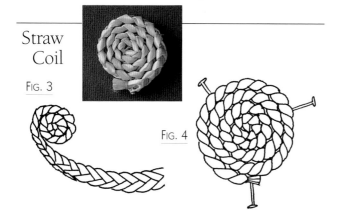

Fig. 3

Fig. 4

Coils are simply plaits that are rolled up into spirals. They can serve as embellishments or, as is the case with the Triskeleon on page 62, as a focal point for an entire project. Three-Straw Hair Braids, Compass Weave plaits, or even the more complicated Seven-Straw FTG plaits can be used; just remember that in order to make a plait of the length required, you'll need to select one to which it's easy to add new straws.

Weave the plait first. Then wrap it snugly around itself, starting at the narrow end, to make a circle (Fig. 3). Avoid pulling on the braid too tightly, or you may pull out new straw inserts or break the braid. When you're finished, secure the coil by stitching the end of the plait in place or inserting one or more straight pins through the coil layers (Fig. 4).

To attach the coil to the project, either glue or stitch it in place.

Straw Flower

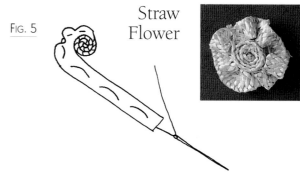

Fig. 5

Actually a variation of the straw coil, this flower consists of a Seven-Straw Ribbon plait. Weave 8" to 10" (20.3 to 25.4 cm) of this plait and tie off each end. Coil up the first half of the plait to create a flower bud. To make the outer petals, first run a gathering stitch along the bottom edge of the remaining length of the braid (Fig. 5). When you're finished, pull the thread to gather this portion and wrap it once around the bud, shaping it as desired. Secure the end of the braid in place by stitching it to the bud. Stitch or glue the finished flower to the project.

Three-Corner Straw Star

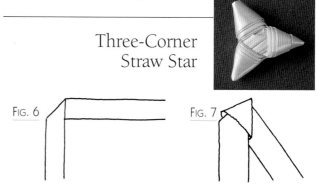

Fig. 6

Fig. 7

The Three-Corner Star is one of the simplest and most striking of embellishments. To make it, you'll need one well-soaked split, with some of the pith scraped off its starch side.

Hold the split horizontally and fold about 1" (2.5 cm) of the left-hand end down to form a right angle (Fig. 6). Now you'll wrap the tip of the fold with the longer end of the split. Bring the longer end of the split around to the left, over the fold, and down underneath it (Fig. 7).

Next, shift the longer split end to lie more directly under the shorter one and turn the weave so that it rests horizontally, with the first point of the star on the left (Fig. 8).

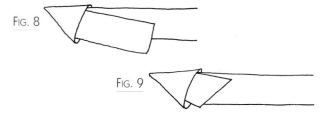

Fig. 8

Fig. 9

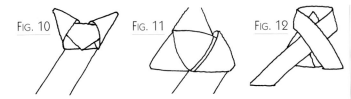

FIG. 10   FIG. 11   FIG. 12

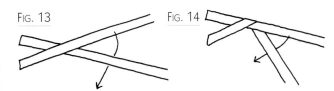

FIG. 13   FIG. 14

To make the second point of the star, first trim the shorter length of the split to the angle shown in Figure 9. Then wrap the long end of the split up, over, and around itself (Fig. 10). The weave should now look like a backward Y-shape.

To create the third and last point of the star, first turn the star so that the first point is at the bottom left. Then wrap the longer end up and around itself (Fig. 11).

You'll notice that you've been working in a clockwise direction. To continue wrapping, turn the star slightly counterclockwise. Bring the longer split end under the first point of the star, and up and over it to wrap it. Turn the star counterclockwise again, and bring the longer split end under, up, and over the next point. Continue to wrap in this fashion. As the points get larger, they'll look more symmetrical and attractive!

When only 1-1/2" (3.8 cm) of split remains, cut the tip to a point and turn the star over. Using Figure 12 as a guide, insert the cut tip under the upper wrap and pull it to lock it in place. Trim the cut end as necessary—and your star is complete. Use glue to attach it to your project.

Swiss Purl Rose

Swiss weavers favor a delicate little rose made with a Purl plait. Tie together seven straws and weave a Three-Purl plait with ten purl sections (or eight if your straws are short). Tie off the end of the plait on the non-purl side and run a gathering stitch along the length of the plait. Pull the gathering thread, coil the plait around itself, and then stitch the bottom edge of the flower to hold the coil together. You may want to pull the purl sections down to accentuate their petal-like appearance. This rose can be stitched or glued onto a project.

Split Straw Rose

The Split Straw Rose, shown at the center of the Circle of Spring on page 125, is a very popular embellishment in contemporary wheat weaving. Start by soaking two straws for 20 minutes. Split them both, and while they're still very damp, wrap them, starch side out, around your finger.

Secure the damp coil with a small clothespin or paper clip and return it to the soaking container until you're ready to work with it.

Unroll the two damp splits. Referring to Figure 13, place one of them in the palm your hand, starch side up. Place the second split on top of the first, starch side down. The center of the cross shape formed by the splits should be about 2" (5.1 cm) from the wider ends of the straws. Fold

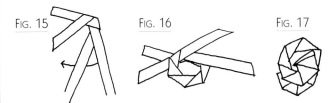

FIG. 15   FIG. 16   FIG. 17

the upper split over the lower split (Fig. 14). Then fold what was the lower split and is now the upper split over the split beneath it (Fig. 15).

Continue to fold the upper split up and over the lower split, turning your work counterclockwise as you work, until you have a six-sided circular shape with a hole in its center (Fig. 16). Keep folding in this fashion, allowing the folded length to develop underneath itself in a spiral shape (Fig. 17). Be sure to leave a small hole in the center of the spiral.

When the split lengths are only 1-1/2" to 2" (3.8 to 5.1 cm) long, push them both—and the short lengths at the beginning of the spiral—down through the hole in the center. To help create the center bud, use a pair of needle-nose pliers to twist the center of the rose. Then, holding the four split ends beneath the rose tightly, turn the petals counterclockwise to open up the geometrically shaped spiral into a more natural pattern.

Tie off the four ends of the splits with thread, just underneath the rose. To attach the rose to a project, either tie or glue it in place.

Adding Other Grains

The natural look of a straw design can often be enhanced by adding grains other than wheat as decorative elements. Delicate oats and wispy rice, for example, will add texture and volume to any project without distracting attention from the overall design.

Acknowledgements

I would like to thank my family—generations past and present—for their love of handiwork, especially wheat weaving, and for having provided me with the ability to take this art form as far as I have. I'm deeply grateful for being able to stand on the shoulders of those from the past as I look forward to the future.

My special thanks go to **Christine Gilbreath**, for helping me to put this book together; **Kelley Jones**, whose illustrations for this book are remarkable visual translations of the text—and of what wheat weaving is all about; **Michael G. Patton**, for his amazing ability to capture special works of art on film; **Chris Rich**, my editor at Lark Books, for her skills and for her appreciation of this art form; **Elaine Thompson**, my art director at Lark, for her sensitive treatment of my subject matter; and **Evan Bracken** (Light Reflections, Hendersonville, NC), for his wonderful photos of the braids and projects.

I'm especially pleased to thank the artists who so graciously made wheat weavings for this book: **Christine Gilbreath** (The Gleaner, page 116); **Donna Hall** (Candle Glow Wreath, page 129); **Cora Hendershot** (Celtic Knot, page 89); **Kelley Jones** (Black Forest Crown, page 5); **Rita Kyser** (Kincardine Maiden, page 54); **Linda Meeker** (Circle of Hearts, page 6); **Kathie Osburn** (Osburn Crown, page 107); and **Marian Vauvra** (Circle of Spring, page 125).

My thanks also go to Darlene Baker, Sharon Hansen, Cora Hendershot, Wendy Johnson, Rita Kyser, Jennifer Landon, Veronica Main, Nonie McFarlane, Marilyn Meador, Nancy Meeker, Bonnie Monzon, and Birgit Wildenhoff for helping to pull material together and for their feedback.

Photo of wheat on endpapers: © Jon Riley

Sources

The following organizations and businesses are invaluable sources of information, supplies, or both:

Amercian Museum of Straw Art
Postal Box 6488
Long Beach, CA 90806

National Association of Wheat Weavers
P.O. Box 344
11208 E. 82nd Avenue
Buhler, KS 67522

Campus Granary
Bethel College Women's Association
North Newton, KS 67117

Black Beards, Ltd.
Sharon and Dennis Hanson
Box 477
Turtle Lake, ND 58575

Sunny Acres Wheat
233 W. Randolph
P.O. Box 218
Howard, KS 67349-0218

Leonie Goodsell
Wylah Farm
104 Katanna Road
Wedderburn, NSW 2560
Australia

Country Straw Pickin's
P.O. Box 44
Frontier
Saskatchewan, SNO OWO
Canada

The Guild of Straw Craftsmen
Crafts Council
44a Pentonville Road
Islington
London N1 9BY
England

Metric Conversion Charts

Inches	CM	Inches	CM	Inches	CM
1/8	0.3	9	22.9	30	76.2
1/4	0.6	10	25.4	31	78.7
3/8	1.0	11	27.9	32	81.3
1/2	1.3	12	30.5	33	83.8
5/8	1.6	13	33.0	34	86.4
3/4	1.9	14	35.6	35	88.9
7/8	2.2	15	38.1	36	91.4
1	2.5	16	40.6	37	94.0
1-1/4	3.2	17	43.2	38	96.5
1-1/2	3.8	18	45.7	39	99.1
1-3/4	4.4	19	48.3	40	101.6
2	5.1	20	50.8	41	104.1
2-1/2	6.4	21	53.3	42	106.7
3	7.6	22	55.9	43	109.2
3-1/2	8.9	23	58.4	44	111.8
4	10.2	24	61.0	45	114.3
4-1/2	11.4	25	63.5	46	116.8
5	12.7	26	66.0	47	119.4
6	15.2	27	68.6	48	121.9
7	17.8	28	71.1	49	124.5
8	20.3	29	73.7	50	127.0

Volumes

1 fluid ounce	29.6 ml
1 pint	473 ml
1 quart	946 ml
1 gallon (128 fl. oz.)	3.785 l

Weights

0.035 ounces	1 gram
1 ounce	28.35 grams
1 pound	453.6 grams

Index to Plaits

Index to Subjects